THE
ASSISTANT
PRINCIPAL
and the Art of
SUCCESSFUL
DEPARTMENT
MANAGEMENT

A HOW-TO GUIDEBOOK FOR SUPERVISORS IN SECONDARY SCHOOLS

HARVEY KRAUT

A|Y
S|A AYSA Publishing, Inc.
Staten Island, New York

SEP -- '04

The Assistant Principal and the Art of Successful Department Management

A How-to Guidebook for Supervisors in Secondary Schools

By Harvey Kraut

Published by: *Aysa Publishing, Inc.*
                 P.O. Box 131556
                 Staten Island, New York 10313 USA
                 Phone & Fax: (718) 370-3201

Printed in the United States of America
Library of Congress Control Number: 2003094639
Kraut, Harvey
The Assistant Principal and the Art of Successful Department Management: A How-to Guidebook for Supervisors in Secondary Schools/by Harvey Kraut
Includes Index
ISBN: 0-9640602-5-6: $19.95 Softcover Canada $25.95

Table of Contents

Brief Version

Table of Contents

About the Author

Mr. Kraut has been in the New York City Public Schools for thirty-three years. He is a licensed Assistant Principal Supervision and Administration and has taught at the university level.

This book is the outcome of the author's decision to share his expertise with those about to embark upon a supervisory career as well as those presently in the position. *The Assistant Principal and the Art of Successful Department Management* is a how-to guide that provides a foundation for administering a secondary school department.

Mr. Kraut earned his BA degree from Indiana University, Bloomington, and both the Masters in History and the Professional Certificate in Administration and Supervision from Brooklyn College of the City University of New York.

Acknowledgment

As with my first book *Teaching and the Art of Successful Classroom Management* the author is again grateful to many for their constructive suggestions, insights and encouragement in bringing this title to publication and without whom this project would not have germinated to bloom.

It is not often that one makes the acquaintance of someone, without the privilege of meeting face-to-face, who repeatedly demonstrates an interest in the work of the other and makes himself available with steadfast assistance. I am indebted to Dr. George J. Petersen, Associate Professor, University of Missouri-Columbia for being such an individual.

To my wife, Joanne, son, Daniel and daughters Lisa and Debbie I give my love and my thanks for their time in reviewing the manuscript.

▓▓▓▓▓▓▓ FOREWORD ▓▓▓▓▓▓▓

In the last two decades we have experienced an unrelenting thrust by state and national legislators, businesses, private organizations and foundations to reform public education in the United States. Most recently, *The No Child Left Behind Act of 2001* requires that school leaders be responsible for enhancing the competencies of their teachers in order to improve student outcomes. As the world of school leadership and policy implementation becomes increasingly more complex, school administrators find themselves attempting to manage numerous transformational imperatives along with competing and often conflicting demands on their time. Clearly, our thoughts about leadership have changed and schools now attempt to be more inclusive through the empowerment of participants with the goal of building learning organizations. Despite the crush of competing agendas, the world's future is inextricably linked to the quality of its schools, its K-12 educators, and the leadership of its administrators. Time and again, research clearly demonstrates that building and district leaders in high performing schools create and sustain a positive district ethos through their relationship with their teachers, staff and members of the community.

This book addresses some of the major leadership and management issues faced by assistant principals, especially those assuming the position for the first time. Students who desire to become school leaders as well as those who prepare them will find the material in this book useful. Current practitioners should also find key dimensions of organizational leadership presented here useful in their application to the "real-world" of practice. The content is for anyone who wants to understand and successfully practice leadership in an educational setting.

This new edition builds on the successful work of Harvey Kraut's *Teaching and the Art of Successful Classroom Management (3rd Edition)*, New York, AYSA. It presents the key dimensions of the assistant principalship gleaned from a wealth of professional experience by the author. Similar to his previous work in the field of education, this book encourages the reader to think about the complex leadership roles of the assistant principal through the lens of practice. Its focus on the small managerial issues to large and substantive leadership responsibilities are presented in a very reader friendly, and almost chronological (first day to end-of-the-year) fashion. In fact, the personal caveats provide an individualized quality permitting the reader to reflect on their personal experiences and perceptions. The vignettes and collected writing in each chapter will assist readers in building a personal and professional knowledge repository as they begin to explore the role of the assistant principal and the important function these administrators provide in the overall leadership of the school.

If the "good old days" in school administration ever existed, they are gone now. Given the national conversation and reports from the field the role and responsibilities of school administrators have shifted from managing a relatively homogeneous student population toward leading a highly specialized, diverse and vastly complex organization. This book offers realistic guidelines to the novice administrator. Through a collection of uncomplicated and well-written chapters, the author provides examples of how to prepare, navigate and succeed in the often turbulent waters of school leadership.

George J. Petersen, Ph.D.
Associate Professor
Educational Leadership and Policy Analysis
University of Missouri-Columbia

WARNING DISCLAIMER

This book was created to provide instruction for Assistant Principals in secondary schools. It is offered solely with the acknowledgement of the buyer that the author and publisher render information only to complement other educational sources. The Assistant Principal is best served by further inquiry into the works of others in administration and supervision in secondary schools.

Effort has been taken in the preparation of this book to make it clear and concise. The book should be viewed as a tool and not as an absolute source of information in the management of an academic/vocational school department.

If you do not wish to be bound by the statement above, please return this book to Aysa Publishing for a refund.

Introduction

Secondary school Assistant Principals (APs) are multi-roled educators! They are seasoned classroom professionals who have ascended the hierarchical ladder to become school management specialists. These individuals head academic and/or vocational departments in secondary schools. They are the middle managers of the school. They function as administrators, mentors to staff, team leaders of the principal's inner-cabinet, guidance consultants, and liaisons to students and their families. In addition, their school-wide involvement makes them important role models for others within the school and the community at large.

APs possess an educational philosophy that sets a foundation for action in meeting school needs. A premise of their philosophy is to develop within each youngster the social, economic, and personal competencies that are necessary for participating in and contributing to change within society. The supervisor perceives the educational process as a focal point for preparing the individual for the world of work, for meeting one's responsibilities and contributing toward the improvement of social conditions.

The No Child Left Behind Act of 2001, signed into law on January 8, 2002, recognizes that "education must be a national priority and a local responsibility." Its principle calling for greater school accountability, with an emphasis on proven teaching methods, present difficult and necessary challenges for APs and school administrators. A primary challenge directly impacting the AP is the need to actively promote teacher quality through training and recruitment. The Assistant Principal is committed to the democratic process. He/she understands that the school is obligated to assist all students with their diverse educational needs. The supervisor is cognizant of the need to foster school-wide change when and where necessary. As such, he/she is obligated to frequently review and revise curriculum that may be antiquated by the changing social conditions resulting from an expanding technological revolution.

These men and women comprehend the broad aims of education. They are knowledgeable in the methodology for attaining educational goals. As administrators of instructional activities, supervisors contribute to the creation of favorable school-wide conditions for learning. As a result of their involvement, the educational process is made progressively more efficient.

The mission of this writer is to offer the secondary school AP, and those preparing to be APs, a suggested overview for achieving educational outcomes. The book is based solely upon the author's personal experience and is free of intent to take a research-based approach in written content. In addition, the book makes no claim to define every aspect of the AP's daily activity. Special concern and consideration has been given to the AP's vital role in teacher preparation. The contents of this text is not to be taken as dogma. Rather, it should be viewed as another vehicle to complement the literature of supervision. Good luck in your careers!

New school construction. The future begins here!

Self-confidence is the first requisite to great undertakings.

Samuel Johnson, poet

Chapter One

My Initiation

"You forgot something," said the Department Chairperson of Mathematics and Science after I entered his office. I offered a courteous "hello" and walked toward an antique-looking wooden teacher's desk that stood in a far corner of Room 428.

"Sorry," I said apologetically. "What did I forget?"

"You must remember to always keep the door closed," he said with a half-hearted grin. "You don't want to hear all that noise in the hall during passing, do you? This office would be full of kids, too, if you didn't lock it all out," he added, pushing the room door closed with a gentle nudge of his fingertips.

The week prior to this event, I was assigned as the Assistant Principal of Supervision and Administration of the Academic

Department. My predecessor had recently left this vocational high school, of about one thousand students, for "greener pastures." As a newly licensed AP with many years of teaching experience, I was given the position of administering a department of fourteen teachers whose specialties were in social studies, the language arts, and foreign languages.

The Academic Department office had been the size of a rather large "broom closet." Upon my predecessor's unexpected, but immediate departure, it was "confiscated" by the principal to fill the school's need for a general store. The principal asked that I be patient until new quarters could be secured to house the Academic Department. I resolved to make the most of what I anticipated to be a bad, but temporary, situation. The thought would not leave me, however, that this somehow was a test of my new title.

My first office was a makeshift portion of the principal's conference room. I quickly adopted an end portion of the long conference room table as my desk. By the third day of the new term, the Academic Department's portion of the conference table held over twenty school memos, some forty pieces of opened and unopened mail, six textbooks, resource materials for two teaching classes, my bulging black attaché case filled with lesson plans, student hand-outs, chalk, and an attendance book. A nearby wall became my bulletin board for two directives requiring my attendance at out-of-school conferences over the next three weeks. In addition to the five or six students standing in the doorway of the conference room each morning waiting to speak to me about school matters, I felt the urgent need to respond to a host of phone calls from parents and the district office. On this third morning, before my arrival to the conference room, an emissary from the program office had discovered enough empty space on my desk to place twenty-three student program-change requests for my attention. I felt as if I were suffocating!

My resignation became a more certain option by the fourth day, when three school secretaries politely asked if they could share the conference table during a morning coffee break. Could I say "no" to such a request? Armed with a variety of snacks in paper bags, the ladies made space for themselves by neatly placing some of my accumulated memos and folded class-room maps on a pile of student records that I planned to review.

That afternoon, I informed the principal that unless he could find office space for the Academic Department, I had no recourse but to resign in view of an impossible work environment. To my surprise, he responded with a calm "O.K." "Share the office with Mr. S. It's large enough to hold both Departments." Relieved that I was about to have office space of my own, I thanked him. As I climbed the four flights of stairs to Room 428, I couldn't help but think, "Now why couldn't he have considered that before?"

The department office that I was to share with Mr. S. housed two wooden teacher desks, a long rectangular conference table, six chairs, and four old metal file cabinets. One entire wall of the room, from floor to ceiling, was filled with science and mathematics texts presumably acquired as complimentary copies from a variety of publishers over many years. Spine to spine they stood out coldly from multi-shelved steel bookcases. Mr. S. "donated" an empty file cabinet with a broken drawer and three bookcase shelves for my department's use. Over a two-day period, I placed about seventy dust-laden science and math texts from the "donated" shelves into several paper cartons. A custodian discarded them a week later.

It was staff knowledge that the Science and Mathematics office was usually closed or unfrequented by department members other than for occasional meetings. To gain admittance, one had to knock about a half-dozen times before the door might slowly open revealing the top of Mr. S.'s head. The narrow opening gave a visitor a brief glimpse into a room that was drab, hostile, and uninviting! Now that I was to share space with Mr. S., how would I function in an environment incompatible with my perception of a department office? Fortunately, an unanticipated event provided a solution.

At the end of my first term as AP, Mr. S. announced his upcoming retirement. I am not certain whether his departure was pre-planned or whether it was my supervisory style that forced him to make this decision. I do remember during that first term frequently being asked by Mr. S. "Why do you do so much preparation in behalf of your staff?" Suffice it to say that his retirement gave me possession of the entire office. The principal, perhaps in atonement for the way I was treated earlier, confided to me one day that Mr. S.'s successor would not confront the hardships that I faced my first term. A new office would be provided for a newly appointed AP of Science and Mathematics. Assured now that my department would possess permanent quarters in the fall, planning for the new school year became more realistic.

My "initiation" as a supervisor is told with the intent of alerting the reader to unanticipated discoveries in the workplace. The supervisor works with others in a capacity much different from his/her former position as "teacher." Frequently, formerly held perceptions have to be reconciled with new realities. Consider a case in point.

In the past, Ms. X, a member of the department, had been part of the staff's daily coffee clique. She was perceived to be personable and professional. As a new AP, I soon discovered other "attributes" of Ms. X. As a teacher she demonstrated a history of frequent lateness, typically failed to meet department deadlines for submitting reports and/or student statistics, and demonstrated a lack of classroom control resulting, at times, in student and parental complaints. As AP, my view of Ms. X changed dramatically; it was with this "altered" image of a colleague that I now had to re-adjust. Thankfully, it didn't take too long to accomplish this.

As a new AP, assume your role as a school leader. Make the need to organize your department an immediate priority. Office readiness is vital to department efficiency; it provides stability in executing supervisory and administrative operations.

Instead of setting numerical quotas, management should work on improvements of the process.

W. Edwards Deming, author

Chapter Two

Taking Stock

The summer break permitted me much needed time. One school term had demonstrated that a department head wore many hats. What I needed most was to clearly find avenues that led to administrative efficiency. I prepared a managerial checklist to help me identify the scope of duties in my departmental operations and to serve me as a guide in identifying problems in need of solution. In that it proved to be an invaluable tool, I submit it for the reader's consideration.

I. Administrative Responsibilities
A. *The Department Office*
1. Space available for staff members
2. Space available for department chairperson
3. Furniture

a) AP's desk
b) conference table
c) chairs
d) file cabinets
e) bookcases
f) computers and software
4. Display materials
   a) bulletin boards
   b) wall decorations
5. Working with the department budget
6. Hiring department personnel
7. Rating personnel
8. Textbook and other purchases
9. Reporting of mandated/special test results to appropriate agencies
10. Preparing for special school events and state/city mandated exams

B. *The Programming Office*
1. Programming classes for the new term; establishing rapport
2. Securing favorable room availability for department teachers in proximity to the Department office
3. Establishing guidelines for student program changes
4. Working with individual student problems and requests
5. Assisting AP colleagues with programming efforts and problems

C. *The Guidance Office*
1. Establishing lines of communication with guidance, deans and attendance personnel
2. Student records; monitoring incoming freshmen and seniors
3. Planning for special student needs; bilingual, handicapped, honors
4. Establishing a recruitment team to feeder schools

D. Member of the Principal's Cabinet
  1. Making recommendations that serve the school efficiently
  2. Implementation of directives from the principal and Board of Education
  3. Acting as the school liaison to Board of Education meetings
  4. Active participant at school-community open houses
  5. Demonstrating department needs in securing fiscal allocations
  6. Preparation for mandated test days

E. Staff Needs
  1. Primary and secondary source materials for classroom lessons
  2. Equipment
     a) classroom display materials; maps, posters, book jackets
     b) overhead projector/related materials
     c) VCR, film, and slide projector
     d) TV
     e) Film, video tapes/slide library; blank video tapes
     f) phonograph, tape recorder, radio
     g) computer equipment and software
  3. Model lesson plans for teachers
  4. Absentee-teacher lesson plans
  5. Teacher supplies
     a) book receipts
     b) attendance books
     c) chalk
     d) erasers
     e) classroom passes
     f) variety of paper
     g) pencils, clips, staples, rubber bands
  6. Calendars of lessons/term outlines, State guidelines and requirements
  7. Uniform homework sheets for classroom distribution
  8. Audio-visual, map, and computer software titles for

teachers.
9. Department course requirements for students
10. Department announcements to parents

F. *Bookroom and Storage areas*
1. Book inventory lists
2. List of outdated books/book shortages
3. Bookroom organization
4. Storage availability/non-book inventory lists
5. Book carts and delivery system
6. Teacher book order/return forms
7. Student book receipt forms

G. *Office Files*
1. Alphabetized book inventory cards
2. Observation reports/teacher profiles
3. Students with special problems folders
4. Model lesson plans
5. Absentee lesson plans
6. Organized rolodex
7. Calendar of lessons/course outlines by subject areas
8. Special projects
9. Intra-school/Guidance Department/Principal communications
10. Board of Education/District Office memos/announcements
11. Home contact forms
12. Uniform homework originals, by subject area, on computer disks
13. Student test results/test statistics
14. Department conference notes
15. Minutes of principal's cabinet meetings
16. School security/safety announcements
17. Duplicated teacher/student materials
18. Opening term course requirements for students
19. Opening term parent notification sheets with acknowledgment cutoffs

20. Introductory department materials for new/novice teachers
21. Instructions for substitute teachers

II. Supervisory Responsibilities

1. Review incoming student records for special needs and placement
2. Establish cooperative links with Guidance and Program Offices regarding course needs, room assignments for courses and teachers, preparation for school-wide test days
3. Establish a teacher conference schedule for a term
4. Set teacher observation timetable
5. Teacher programming
6. Subject class programming
7. Evaluate present course offerings/new course proposals
8. Responsibilities as a member of Principal's cabinet
9. Staff development conferences
10. Individual teacher/student meetings
11. List office periods on department door
12. Writing observation reports

III. Community Outreach

1. Department newsletter
2. Review/rewrite home notices
3. Establish liaison with local police department
4. Prepare for parent-teacher conferences/Open School Week
5. Arranging community speaker visitations
6. Preparation for out-of-school class visitations

The checklist offers the Assistant Principal (also referred to as the AP, chairperson, Chair, or supervisor), an overview of his/her multi-faceted responsibilities. In some instances there may be an obvious overlap of administrative and supervisory functions. However, preparing a list serves as a first step toward sound office management.

Launching the first department conference. There just weren't enough days of summer to accomplish all that I wanted to do in preparation for my second new school term. I managed, however, to achieve several goals from my summer list of "things to do." The week prior to the new term, I arrived early one morning with an attaché case of materials to be duplicated. I was aware that department members should actively participate in the development of curriculum and materials, but time had been too short during the first term to properly organize staff committees. I needed a fresh start in launching the new term. Staff input, therefore, was placed temporarily on hold but not forgotten.

Among the items I duplicated for the opening of the term were,

1. A "Conference Agenda" for the first meeting with department staff.
2. Department textbook, slide, film, and software lists.
3. "Uniform homework" master packets for four different social studies offerings.
4. Department course requirements for students.
5. Opening term announcements, with tear-off slips, for parents.
6. Three initial absentee lesson plans, for distribution to each staff member, in case of an emergency absence. These lessons were skills-oriented so that they would meet the needs of all students.

The opening meeting (school for students had not yet officially begun) with members of my department went smoothly. I brought a large coffeemaker from home, along with a box of donuts from a nearby store, for the first staff meeting of the term. The materials I prepared were well received by the social studies teachers who, at the appropriate time, took class sets of the uniform homework that were made available for distribution.

The "Conference Agenda" became a fulcrum for discussion of school and department issues. After I set the stage for a topic, a staff volunteer led the discussion. I sat to one side of the room taking notes of conference comments. I observed that individuals who rarely participated during former meetings of the department now contributed to the discussion. The atmosphere was one of calm and friendly interaction.

Near the termination of the conference, I asked for assistance in evolving an agenda for future conference topics. Teachers were asked to meet in groups of three or four for the purpose of selecting topics they felt important for discussion. After several minutes, groups presented their choices. I requested volunteers from the groups to become team leaders for drafting future agendas. These agendas would be submitted, to me, prior to the department's monthly meetings. Each group was informed that it would lead a conference during the term.

Educational objectives. Secondary school supervisors have a personal educational philosophy for achieving school goals. The supervisor is a key participant who provides direction to the school's effort for educating young people. Further, he/she supports goals that seek to assist students in preparing them for their place in society. These educational goals are

1. The development of character.
2. Understanding the American heritage.
3. Establishing social relationships.
4. Acquiring skills for research.
5. Learning to respect one's body and maintaining it in good health.
6. Preparing for an occupation.
7. Acquiring the necessary knowledge to meet the needs of a changing global economy.
8. An appreciation for the environment and an understanding of its limitations.
9. Developing critical thinking skills.

10. To seek guidance avenues for resolving personal problems.

The AP helps shape the educational preparation of youngsters. He/she is aware of differing intellectual needs, abilities, and interests. A primary role is to provide instructional and guidance services with prudence and efficacy. A secondary aim of this writer is to present a pragmatic approach for leading a secondary school department.

Be willing to make decisions. That's the most important quality in a good leader. Don't fall victim to what I call the ready–aim-aim-aim-aim syndrome.

T. Boone Pickens, businessman

Chapter Three

Developing Positive Supervisor-Teacher Relationships

An important ingredient for attaining school objectives is the enhancement of relationships among department heads, students and staff. The AP, not unlike the teacher, is firm but fair, pragmatic in dealing with suggestions and criticism, demonstrates an ability to act constructively, and assumes the role of leadership under a banner of democratic cooperation.

Factors affecting supervisor-teacher relations. The first of four factors affecting supervisor-teacher relations is the environment within the school; those conditions that are central to persistent problems, tensions, and morale that concern teachers. The second hinges on the role and level of understanding, or degrees of friction, between the supervisor and teacher perceptions involving action of choice and accountability. Third, is the degree of background disparity between the AP and staff members in terms of sex, age, race, social values, and attitudes. The fourth factor relates to the social and professional standing of teacher groups and individuals whose demeanor enhances either school or department unity or conflict.

The supervisor is cognizant of those factors that affect relationships. It is his/her responsibility to channel department members toward an environment of mutual cooperation. The quest for cooperation rallies around those elements that reduce friction in the workplace. The AP is patient in affecting change that narrows, rather than excludes, professional disharmony. He/she creates an aura of tolerance and reconciliation that bridges professional differences with common interests. The chairperson demonstrates goodwill in the daily involvement of department personnel. This does not mean that he/she fails to act in accordance with managerial responsibilities required of his/her position.

Striving toward department harmony. The democratic supervisor understands that there are limitations upon department democracy. Teachers, for example, are not in authority to dictate policy by majority rule. Situations involving school safety, security and orders from superiors to take imperative and immediate school action make democratic supervision relative. Absolute democracy is not plausible because of limitations posed by novice and/or weak teachers, arid individual attitudes and the unwillingness, by some, for cooperation in the workplace.

An issue that frequently poses a problem for a newly appointed AP is professional intolerance by older more experienced teachers toward novice colleagues. Some "old-timers" approaching retirement, perhaps "burned out" by daily routine, are often uncomfortable in an atmosphere of a novice teacher's enthusiasm for teaching. Among veteran instructors there may be those who are embittered by repeated unsuccessful efforts to move up the career ladder. Such teachers may view teaching as just a "9-5 job;" one lacking in mobility and job satisfaction. In these situations the chairperson needs to tread carefully in his/her quest for department harmony. Yet, he/she remains cognizant that among several, or all these individuals, a wealth of experience exists to be shared with others.

As a new department head, I confronted such a dilemma. Of fourteen department staff members, five had over twenty years of teaching experience. Of the remaining nine, three were newly arrived to the profession, and six had less than four years of classroom exposure. I weighed my options in trying to unite all into a common professional cause.

In search of a solution, I adopted a "coffee cup" approach to problem solving. During a teacher's free period, each of five experienced teachers was invited to join me for coffee. At the meeting, casual conversation moved toward the need to help "our" novice teachers. I spoke with each instructor of his/her positive contributions to the department, and asked each for assistance in mentoring a novice teacher. If my request was honored, inter-visitation arrangements were made for a novice teacher so that he/she could observe the classroom strategies of an experienced mentor. The five veterans proved to be sympathetic and cooperative. In the months that followed, my spot-check observations indicated that the "buddy system" was of considerable importance in aiding the professional growth of our novice teachers. Follow-up inquiries, to both mentors and novices, confirmed my perceptions.

The typical secondary school frequently needs teachers to fill partial non-teaching assignments such as attendance coordinator, a member of the program committee, grade advisor, dean, and crisis intervention counselor. In school districts bound by teacher unions and Boards of Education contracts, there are specific rules and regulations involving school-wide seniority rights for non-teaching positions. As a member of the Principal's inner-cabinet, I had input in the selection of able candidates.

Aside from recognizing particular contractual obligations, input in the selection of a candidate for a non-teaching assignment rests on the principle of fairness as indicated by the progress made in one's professional growth. Obviously, one cannot please everyone; my selection decision was motivated solely by professional considerations and not by any personal relationship with a particular individual.

The department conference. The department conference is an important vehicle for communicating and disseminating professional information. It serves the AP as an opportunity for creating an aura conducive to the free exchange of individual and group expression. Democratic leadership permits rapport with others through the avenue of cooperative staff planning. The chairperson, by providing both administrative and supervisory support to department efforts, assists in strengthening bonds in the AP-staff partnership. In offering teachers security, openness, and a commitment to act on decisions mutually arrived at, the supervisor demonstrates respect for others and permits the vehicle of democratic supervision to enhance morale and to strengthen the bonds of working relationships.

In that the department conference serves staff members as a forum for active participation, it is not to be dominated by the AP. Generally, an upcoming conference is pre-announced, permitting the staff time to "digest" the proposed agenda. Pre-conference notification is easily accomplished by placing agenda copies into staff mailboxes.

At our conferences, administrative matters were announced at either the opening or end of the meeting. Administrative information was presented and, if possible, quickly brought to conclusion. I tried to establish a cordial but professional atmosphere believing that this enhanced staff perception that the conference was "for them." The final conference minutes reflected opinions of staff contributors. I forwarded memos of appreciation to conference contributors to augment the supervisor-teacher relationship.

Conference goals. The goals of a department conference are many, of which the more obvious are:

1. To discuss and motivate activities of common concern to members.
2. To establish an environment for the open exchange of information.
3. To investigate and consider instructional methodology and resource materials based upon new research findings.
4. To offer assistance in handling specific pedagogical and/or school problems.
5. To improve teacher morale and to strengthen the supervisor-teacher dialogue.
6. To create an environment of cooperation in establishing and achieving department goals.

At our second department meeting, the conference opened with several administrative announcements followed by a handout of topics for future meetings that had been selected by the mini-committees. Next to a topic were the names of committee members, the leader volunteer, and the date of their future conference. Team leaders had been informed to submit a brief agenda, to me, for duplication prior to a committee-led conference.

There were four additional meetings that second term. Once a teacher-led conference was launched, and administrative announcements completed, I sat to one side of the department office or of a classroom made available for the meeting. I learned to become a good listener! Listening carefully to others reveals "clues" to their thinking. This requires an ability to concentrate, while taking notes. As an individual spoke, I wrote short phrases or key words to remember specific items. Issues that were in need of clarification were also recorded. At the end of each meeting, I summarized briefly, at the bottom of my note-taking sheet, key points. Good listening technique produced important results! First, it reflected my interest in what others had to say. Secondly, it helped me to not overlook pertinent ideas and provided my staff with the opportunity to consider items that I addressed. By initiating teacher involvement in discussion activities and committing myself to act upon mutually arrived staff recommendations I strengthened department relationships.

At the end of our conference, I elicited a staff summary that was written on the chalkboard. A volunteer secretary included the summary into the official minutes of the meeting. When time restraints prohibited a finalized conference outcome, the presentation committee carried over specific items to the next conference. At that conference, unresolved issues were reviewed, discussed, and followed up with written staff recommendations, presented to me a day or two later for approval. When approved, conference issues were presented at the principal's cabinet meeting. If I had disapproved a recommendation, it was returned to the committee for reconsideration and revision.

Evaluating the conference. I evaluated each conference for its specifics! Did the meeting accomplish intended objectives? Were the objectives clearly defined? Was there active participation? Did the conference create a tone that permitted the free exchange of ideas? Was there cohesiveness between the last and earlier conferences? Did teachers feel that the meeting was of professional interest? Did the conference stimulate teacher thinking about the topics at hand?

To secure responses to any or all of these questions, I would place a questionnaire into staff mailboxes requesting feedback. In that experimentation with new classroom strategies were encouraged, a frequent reminder was attached to the questionnaire requesting an invitation to informally observe any innovative classroom experience that was going well. When a teacher responded to my inquiry, I wrote a brief note of "appreciation" to that individual. I often spoke with staff members on a one-to-one basis to assess personal feelings regarding conference suggestions. In that the department conference is only one of several vehicles available to the AP for educational change, let us turn our attention to other responsibilities of the supervisor.

Example is not the main thing in influencing others. It is the only thing.

Albert Schweitzer, philosopher, theologian

Chapter Four

The Staff Development Program

A child's success in school is related to the instruction of well-prepared and qualified teachers who demonstrate command of their subject and have the ability to institute methods and techniques of instruction that create an environment for learning and stimulate students to become active participants in the classroom. In addition, these teachers have the capability of getting youngsters to internalize information for both present and future use.

The *No Child Left Behind Act 2001*, (NCLB) requires that teachers in core academic areas meet the requirement of being "highly qualified" by the conclusion of the 2006 school year. A teacher will have to be the recipient of a bachelor's degree, be licensed by his/her state, and demonstrate competence in a subject area of concentration. APs will be accountable for enhancing teacher preparation and competency in the classroom. The NCLB Act provides school districts with flexibility for finding new and innovative methods to improve teacher quality. It will be essential for the AP to provide leadership and training for non-traditional educational personnel making a transition from other vocations into teaching. This will include the need to work with qualified paraprofessionals and to assist them in preparing for and achieving teacher certification. This is no simple task! It will challenge APs and administrators to be creative in transforming novice instructors into master teachers.

Aim of good class management. Class management may be defined as the organization of the physical and human elements of the instructional environment. It is a means to effective learning! Good class management serves many purposes. The instructional goal for establishing an orderly environment is to achieve an atmosphere conducive for students to learn and to have them acquire personal traits for self-discipline, responsibility, positive attitudes toward group undertakings, respect for authority, and efficient work routines. By minimizing the potential for classroom problems, the instructor is able to devote maximum time for student learning.

Under conditions common to an urban school setting, class management routines may be observed as a duality. The first requires teacher awareness and action in preparation of instruction; the need for appropriate lighting, ventilation, a comfortable room temperature, cleanliness, attendance taking, responses to emergency situations, and a simple but structured class dismissal policy. The second duality relates to differing and special needs of the "homeroom" when they exist as part of school-wide operations, and the subject classroom.

The physical condition of the classroom is important because of the stimulating effect it has on youngsters. Good lighting, adequate ventilation, room temperature, and room tidiness all impact the learning environment. A classroom dressed with decorative materials, desk furniture orderly arranged, washed chalkboards in preparation for the first lesson and prepped clean for others instill within students the feeling that this place is their "home away from home." The teacher must also be cognizant of audibility problems created by room size, its location, hazards, and storage needs. An instructor's uncluttered desk offers students the perception that the teacher has taken care of "old business" and is ready to begin anew.

The teacher is primary for instituting positive management procedures. Personal experience has demonstrated that the degree of instructional success is related to structured, although adaptable to variations of lesson content, management techniques designed with inclusion of preventive discipline measures. Organized management routines in subject classes are pivotal for successful instruction and socialization. These routines, however, vary with differences in the maturity level of students and the experience, competence, personality, and teaching style of the instructor.

The supervisor's role in establishing class management routines. The AP is a role model in creating effective classroom management routines. He/she understands the role of managed instructional activities for achieving objectives. The supervisor is aware of strengths and shortcomings relating to the physical conditions of the school, key functions of various school offices, personnel and administrative policies. This knowledge permits the AP to assist teachers in securing needed information. The supervisor, as an instructional leader, encourages his/her staff to focus on sound class management as necessary for effective instruction.

The Assistant Principal anticipates a variety of teacher needs that correlate with their class management. Ideally, the department stock room has a supply of record keeping books needed by teachers for maintaining daily attendance and student performance records, workable audio-visual equipment, a film-audio library, and textbooks that are current and adequate in number so that every youngster has a copy for home use. In addition, there are one or two class sets of texts available for immediate in school needs. The AP also maintains an inventory timetable so that materials in short supply are reordered quickly.

I created Excel files to monitor stockroom items such as textbooks, visual aids, and computer programs. This permitted me control and rapid access over department resources. A teacher's sign-out "log" for films, tapes, maps and visual aids necessary for instruction, allowed me to locate borrowed materials quickly. To expedite the return of materials, and to assist and train teachers in using audio-visual aids, I initiated an A-V squad of youngsters who were rewarded with "quid pro quo" recommendations for college and jobs.

I instructed my teachers in how-to routines that fostered preventive discipline measures in their classrooms, during our department conferences. Department members were coached in instructional planning, lesson timing, and maintaining student performance, attendance, and punctuality records. The staff was habituated with the process of textbook distribution at the beginning of a term and book collection at a term's end. Department policy regarding use of the classroom pass, student cutting, commendation mechanisms, reports to parents, and the issuance of report cards were updated, modified when necessary, and instituted. Teachers were instructed in the chains of command for guidance and administrative aid when in need of assistance with problems beyond their classroom boundaries.

I was the overseer of classroom activities and monitored teacher routines for their impact on role responsibilities; when teacher classroom routines fail to create role characteristics, conflict is a result. A case in point!

The teacher who greets students daily with a brief "good morning" can establish rapport that leads to a positive learning climate. The instructor, however, who greets students at the classroom door engaging several in small talk, while others mull about the room, does not understand preventive discipline routines. In the latter case, the result is that lesson development is curtailed by the instructor's self-imposed limitation upon lesson timing. This raises a question as to whether such an instructor perceives his/her role as a "friend," rather than a "teacher," of young people.[1]

---

[1] Kraut, Harvey, *Teaching and the Art of Successful Classroom Management: A How-to Guidebook for Teachers in Secondary Schools*, (Aysa Publishing, Inc: New York, 2000)

Preparing the novice teacher for the classroom. The majority of novice teachers enter their first classroom encounter armed with a methodology from various sources. This often creates for the teacher a state-of-mind best described as one of confusion. The supervisor is obligated to assist the novice with the necessities for getting his/her classes under way so that the instructor does not feel as if he/she is cast into an arena comparable to an ordeal under fire. So that an inexperienced teacher may enter the classroom with both confidence and direction, the AP must devote considerable time in preparing this individual for the classroom.

The AP desires that a novice teacher have a positive start on which to build teaching experience. He/she instructs new staff members with a methodology for classroom management that limits student disciplinary problems. This does not mean that the AP acts dictatorially or that he/she seeks to impose his/her own methodology upon others. Experienced teachers know that no single methodology is absolute; many have their own proven classroom management techniques. Yet, it is important that an inexperienced instructor be given a tested methodology that can lead to operational success. Having "tools" necessary for launching daily instruction permits the inexperienced instructor to enter the classroom free of the fear of not knowing what to do until he/she is able to personalize a management style based upon his/her classroom experience. What follows is a strategy that offers the novice an ability to launch classroom operations.

Beginning of the classroom period. Assume that a previous period has ended. The teacher and his/her class are coming together from other rooms. Upon entering the room, the teacher places his/her belongings on the desk, takes the daily lesson plan to the chalkboard and writes "Aim:" with a lesson number above it. Teachers with a penmanship problem, or those who find it difficult writing upon the chalkboard, should be informed of the option of using an overhead projector if convenient to do so. This classroom tool offers a new teacher the added advantage of not having to turn his/her back to the class, thereby averting problems.

New teachers frequently have writing problems when first using the chalkboard. I recall one teacher who had an acceptable handwriting but whose prose on the chalkboard formed a near 45-degree angle to the board's frame. Borrowing a chalkboard stylus from the school's Music Department, with five sticks of chalk protruding from its five holders (music teachers use this to draw lines for writing musical notes on the chalkboard), I offered it to the novice as a temporary writing aid. It worked! After a month of continuous use, the teacher's chalkboard writing improved and he no longer needed the stylus.

Next, the teacher places the day's homework, or nightly assignment, at the far right front chalkboard as noted by the following model:

Homework
Class: Am. Hist.2
Do: Assignment #21
Due: Wed., 4/2/02
Reminder: Short quiz next Tues. covering
in-class lessons #18-24 & homework
18-24

The instructor returns to the first board with the noted inscription, "Aim." He/she informs the class that "all notebooks are open and everyone is copying from the front boards." At this point the lesson's Aim has not yet been written on the chalkboard. There is a reason for this. The lesson's Aim is to be elicited from the class at some point during the instructional period and then placed upon the board. This is done to assure the youngsters' attention and to keep them focused upon the lesson's development. However, experience has demonstrated that this pedagogic operation can be somewhat difficult, especially for a beginning instructor, depending upon the academic mix of the class population. If students are academically poor in basic communication skills, the teacher can still succeed in eliciting the lesson's Aim from the class by using content questions that relate to student needs. In such a class, eliciting the Aim directly from youngsters is vital toward uplifting instruction; it challenges weaker students to perform at a level of higher thought.

Motivational device. Beneath the "Aim" is a motivational device. The motivation may consist of almost any "vehicle" that puts students into a frame of mind for the lesson. It may be a quote, a set of instructions to do something, a stick figure cartoon, a series of pictures or photographs along the chalkboard ledge, or a stimulating review question that bridges past lessons with the one for the day.

Beneath the "Aim" the teacher identifies the motivation for the class. To do so he/she might use such terms as "Warm up" or "Do Now." The teacher is encouraged to place the motivational question, instructions, or other device here. The board now has an "Aim," a "Warm up" and the day's homework assignment. As the class copies the front boards, the teacher is ready for the next step. He/she is free to take the daily attendance without disruption. Once attendance taking is completed, school-wide announcements are made if there are any. The teacher is informed to speak briefly in motivating the daily homework assignment and in reminding the class of upcoming tests, quizzes, reports, or other classroom events.

Homework collection. A teacher cannot in all honesty collect homework from each of five classes [this usually is the case for teachers in large American urban secondary schools] and painstakingly grade student papers four or five times per week. It is too grueling a task and a teacher would have little time for family and personal recreation. Rather, students are made aware that the teacher has adopted a system in which daily homework is collected from scattered rows. Students are informed that they can be certain that homework so collected will be performance graded. The instructor explains the collection procedure to the class as follows:

"After attendance is taken, I will ask who did not do last night's homework. Students who have attempted the homework but did not complete it because of some difficulty with it will not be penalized. You must show me proof of your efforts. If you did not do it, you must inform me of this before I announce those rows from which homework will be collected. This includes students who have been absent, unless they brought a parental excuse note. If I am not notified of missing homework, and I call your row for collection, you will be marked for both the missing homework and for failing to inform me of it."

The aforementioned student-confessional is valuable in that it serves to strengthen the teacher's need to teach trustworthiness as a social value. By establishing honesty as a value in the classroom, experience has demonstrated that the majority of students will hereafter oblige the teacher with a show of hands when homework is not done. There will be a few, however, who early in the term will test both the instructor and the procedure. The teacher will most likely discover, as the term progresses, that when a youngster is caught without homework, he/she is often "ridiculed" by the class.

The teacher does not accept an excuse from a student for not having done homework. He/she is marked accordingly in the record book. Once the entire class knows that the instructor "means business," by being consistent in his/her classroom management, students will act more responsibly. The above procedure should be "digested" thoroughly by the novice teacher. They provide for classroom order! Once the teacher has "routinized" the aforementioned steps, youngsters will come to view him/her as the efficient leader of their classroom. The so-called "teaching battle" is half won at this point.

Room appearance. The classroom should also reflect the teacher's content area. A "Current Events" bulletin board should be displayed at a convenient location in the room to which one is assigned for the majority of the daily teaching assignments. Similarly, the room should reflect student papers that demonstrate good test scores, writing samples, drawings, and other academic accomplishments. At a minimum, the teacher should demonstrate a positive sample of each student's performance once during the term. He/she should make the room pleasing to the eye and comfortable to be in so that students will think of this classroom as a "second home." Social studies and language arts instructors, for example, could use newsmagazine covers, bookjackets, and/or posters from travel agencies for their classrooms. One method of securing interesting display materials is by communicating with foreign embassies. Many embassies are pleased to forward materials for classroom use. Teachers of science, mathematics, foreign languages and other subjects can secure materials from organizations in their respective academic or vocational areas. A bulletin board or displays section should also be created for the posting of school and/or guidance announcements.

Differences among teachers. The AP is concerned with the professional growth of each teacher in his/her department. He/she knows that teachers perform differently in the classroom. Differences can be attributed to such complex human factors as intelligence, emotional stability, adaptability, health, and an aptitude for interacting with people. These differences often pose special interpersonal problems for the chairperson.

The AP adopts a clinical approach for identifying personnel problems within the department. He/she understands that individual problems are usually symptomatic of cause and effect relationships. As such, he/she considers a teacher's length of service as a probable focus of teaching problems; is the teacher in question new to the school, new to teaching, or perhaps a classroom veteran who has lost teaching enthusiasm as his/her retirement approaches? In addition, is there information that the individual in question might share with the AP regarding a problem of health, family, or financial hardship that could offer insight in resolving difficulties with instruction?

As a teacher, I understand that words alone do not define "who is a teacher." Yet, a tendency exists in classifying teachers in stereotypical terms; "Mr. W is colorless in his teaching methodology," "Ms. X is a lazy teacher who is capable of inspiring youngsters but doesn't care to do so," "Mr. Y is a superior classroom teacher," "Ms. Z is an inexperienced teacher and has much to learn." Tags label human beings rather than define who they are.

Instructional problems can be recognized as originating from root causes in any one, or all, of four categories: a teacher's length of service, his/her temperament, classroom management, and personal problems. For instructional purposes only, let us identify several teacher "types," by their stereotypical "tags," to demonstrate how the AP might interact with each.

The "unmotivated" teacher. This tag is associated with the teacher frequently perceived as doing minimally in the classroom. For such a teacher, volunteerism, also, is a "not for me" activity. The instructor may also be referred to as a "clock watcher;" one who rarely revises lesson plans, is tactless in student testing, grading papers and evaluating homework.

I have assisted such teachers by involving them in a variety of activities. A teacher might be asked to lead a department meeting, or speak at one, on a topic of educational interest. This often helps him/her to achieve renewed feelings of self-esteem. I also encouraged the instructor to experiment with new learning activities and/or team-teach in the attempt to stimulate his/her creativity and interest. I have also asked some to be "buddies" to novice teachers and to advise them with their classroom difficulties.

The "undemocratic" teacher. This teacher is noted by his/her "feelings" of classroom insecurity. These feelings usually are attributable to one or more underlying causes. This instructor may view the process of education as merely being a transmittal of information rather than the development of values and skills. He/she also may fear an environment that permits open discussion of ideas resulting, regrettably, in the teacher's placing limitations upon student speech.

The supervisor can help this instructor by demonstrating his/her own role as a democratic teacher. The teacher is asked to observe several of the supervisor's classes. Prior to an observation, a brief teacher-AP meeting is held to assist the instructor in identifying democratic features of the AP's classroom instruction. At a post-lesson follow-up, the teacher evaluates the AP's success, or lack of it, in achieving anticipated classroom democratization. The AP's informal, but frequent, observation of this teacher is ongoing. To maximize the teacher's exposure to a variety of instructional environments, the Chair establishes, with approval of other instructors, a schedule for inter-visitations. The assigned teacher references the democratic values he/she has observed, for later discussion with the Chair, with a critique of each classroom visit.

Good teaching is crucial to student success!

The "ineffectual" or "weak" teacher. This instructor is weak in maintaining classroom order and good lesson preparation. The teacher's instructional style may be described as "hit and run," often resulting in a failure to cover lesson content.

To assist this teacher, I would undertake a series of meetings with him/her early in a term. Time would be spent reviewing lesson planning, the ingredients of good classroom management, and preventive discipline, questioning technique, use of the chalkboard, and eliciting lesson Aims and summaries from students. Assistance would not produce dramatic change overnight, but experience demonstrates that small "steps" do inspire teacher motivation and instructional progress. There would be frequent informal/formal and pre and post observation conferences to reevaluate teacher strengths and weaknesses.

The "on the fringe of retirement" teacher. This teacher, most likely, has been in a school system for many years but appears to have lost his/her enthusiasm for the classroom. The teacher is not overly concerned with self-image in the classroom. The instructor merely appears to be awaiting retirement eligibility.

When confronted by such a teacher, I would seek to capitalize upon his/her classroom experience. Calling upon my human relations skills, I would attempt to convince the instructor that his/her many years of experience could make an invaluable contribution to the professional development of others. I would identify the teacher's strengths and ask his/her assistance in helping others.

The "inexperienced" teacher. This teacher is noted by his/her high motivation but lacks classroom experience to be effective. He/she does not fully understand the ingredients of good lesson planning or for establishing a classroom environment with preventive discipline measures. He/she measures teaching success by "trial and error" results. This instructor lacks good questioning skills and an experienced ability to motivate youngsters. As with the "ineffectual" or "weak" teacher, I would pursue a similar program for improvement.

The "superior" teacher. The superior teacher is distinguished by his/her classroom success. This instructor, too, is recognized by a high-level of motivation, a willingness to take risks with innovative learning techniques, demonstrates a positive grasp of classroom management skills, offers students a variety of instructional formats, and demonstrates command of subject content. In addition, the teacher demonstrates rapport with young people and has gained the respect of both students and colleagues. This teacher should also be encouraged to make professional contributions at staff development conferences. I would demonstrate my sincerity in wanting to assist him/her to achieve professional advancement.

The "doubtful" or "unsatisfactory" teacher. No teacher is considered "unsatisfactory" because of poor instructional skills alone. A teacher may be considered unsatisfactory only when the supervisor fairly concludes that an assistance plan has failed because of the instructor's lack of cooperation, inaction, or ability to perform as a classroom professional. An unsatisfactory rating is assigned a teacher only after his/her long-term failure, in spite of ongoing assistance, to achieve performance objectives. It is important when working with a "doubtful" or "unsatisfactory" individual, that the supervisor carefully anecdote all vitae concerning the individual. Documentation includes copies of lesson plans, memos, observation reports, and description of the remediation services provided to the instructor by the AP.

Using teaching tools effectively!

Teaching should be full of ideas, not stuffed with facts.

John Condry, educator

Chapter Five

The Observation Process

Preparing for the classroom observation. The classroom observation is a vital element of teacher supervision. For this occasion, the supervisor plans carefully. The primary goal of an observation is to determine whether a teacher demonstrates professional growth in the classroom. The AP prepares an observation timetable cognizant with his/her total supervisory program. Scheduling is planned for pre and post-observation conferences; the classroom observation is the fulcrum for evaluating teaching skills. At the pre-and post-observation conferences, supervisor/teacher/student needs are addressed. An additional outcome of the observation is helping teachers to evaluate their instructional strengths and weaknesses. The visits also offer the AP a perspective of instructional problems, observable academic abilities of students, and of the physical conditions of classrooms. It also assists the chairperson in appraising teachers for retention/dismissal, promotion, and consideration for special assignments.

Teacher apprehension of the observation process is real and the degree of teacher anxiety produced by it is not to be underestimated. Many instructors perceive the observation as a pro forma administrative device for maintaining "tabs" on personnel. As a result, teacher acceptance of the observation process, as a learning tool, is diminished. It is incumbent upon the AP to address this negative teacher perception, thereby enhancing staff morale and uplifting instruction.

Types of supervisory visits. The number of annual classroom visits to a teacher depends upon the Chair's objectives. In many school districts across the nation, the observation report is required of probationary, substitute, and regularly tenured teachers. The AP in large urban centers is obligated by the Boards of Education to visit newly appointed teachers and assigned regular substitutes three times each term. Veteran and tenured teachers are minimally visited once a term. This regulation may vary from locale to locale. The required visit, for the purpose of observing and evaluating classroom operations and culminating in a written report, is undertaken for an entire instructional period. In instances where instruction appears "weak" or "unsatisfactory," a teacher may be observed more frequently. When planning for a class visit, I first reviewed his/her previous observation reports, written communications to the teacher, and his/her statistical class reports. If my observation was to be pre-announced, I placed a brief memo in the teacher's school mailbox informing him/her of time, place, and class section to be observed.

The pre-and post-observation conference. Prior to a formal observation, I requested a pre-observation conference with the teacher. At the pre-observation conference the instructor and I discussed the upcoming lesson. The teacher's lesson plan was reviewed for its Aim, motivation, materials to be used, and lesson development. We reviewed the lesson's time frame for attaining its objectives. The teacher and I strove toward mutual understanding of lesson particulars so that his/her performance could be measured in achieving objectives.

A post-observation conference followed the observation. Ideally, the meeting occurred within 48-72 hours of the observation. At the conference, the teacher and I discussed the lesson for its specifics. My report followed this meeting.

Lesson analysis. The supervisor is familiar with the process of lesson analysis. As an experienced teacher, he/she is knowledgeable of the instructional components needed for establishing a positive learning environment. During an observation, the AP evaluates the lesson's instructional components. Has an "Aim" been elicited from the class and does the motivation set the stage for lesson development? Has the teacher assigned homework, is it meaningful and placed on the board for all to see? Has attendance been taken? Has there been a lesson review and did the teacher prepare a foundation for new content? Have preliminary and pivotal questions been linked to student experiences? Did the instructor pursue the arrow of recitation and enhance socialization and the teacher-student dialogue? Did the instructor make effective use of the chalkboard to note lesson summaries and were written statements clear and in logical sequence?

Because one cannot recall everything during an observation the AP needs to incorporate a method for objective reporting. To aid him/her, an observation checklist is prepared prior to a classroom visit. This checklist contains key lesson components, with adequate writing space beneath each, to record observations. What follows is a checklist model that could be used as an observation reference.

Observation Checklist

Teacher Name_____   Date_____
Subject & Class Level:_____   Room:_____
Class:_____ Register_____ No. Students Absent:_____

Class Management: _____
_____.

Teacher traits: _____
_____
_____.

Aim: _____
_____
_____.

Motivation: _____
_____
_____.

Homework: _____
_____
_____.

Lesson development:
       preliminary questioning

_____
_____
_____.

medial summary_____
_____
_____.

pivotal questioning_____
_____
_____.

final summary_____
_____
_____.

effective use of chalkboard_____
_____
_____.

socialization & chain of recitation_____
_____
_____.

lesson timing & organizational flow_____
_____
_____.

To this list may be added additional lesson components that the AP doesn't wish to overlook. The checklist is a worksheet for observing instructional classroom specifics.

Observing the classroom environment. Ideally, the supervisor arrives at the door of the teacher's classroom, for a formal observation, a minute or two before class begins. An early arrival permits the observer to witness student entry and early interaction with the teacher. In addition, there are other observations to note at the start of the period. Did youngsters take their seats and open their notebooks with minimum fanfare? Did the instructor demonstrate grasp of classroom priorities? Did he/she succeed in placing the word "Aim" on the chalkboard, introduce a motivational device, and place a homework assignment upon the front board? Was daily attendance taken, homework collected, if any, in a systematic manner? Were school-wide announcements made, if any, and were students informed of any upcoming exams, quizzes, or papers due? Was an "Aim" eventually elicited from the class and placed on the chalkboard? Was it formulated with class interest, relevant and personalized by the use of a pronoun such as "we" or "you?" The motivation consists of almost any "vehicle" that puts students into a frame of mind for the lesson. It may be a quote, a set of instructions to do something, the distribution of a reading selection or handout, a stick figure cartoon, a series of pictures or photographs along the chalkboard ledge or a stimulating review question bridging past lessons with the one for the day. Teachers have been known to "go the extra mile" in their creativity by dressing as historical or fictional characters in order to become lesson focal points. Such motivations, although commendable in their intent, do not necessarily meet the needs of most teachers. What is important is that the motivation act as a source of classroom stimulation that links lesson content, development, and summary with the instructional "Aim."

The homework assignment. As an experienced teacher, the AP appreciates the role of homework in the learning process. Homework assists students to develop study habits that prepare them for independence in learning. Homework permits growth in written expression and in familiarizing students with a methodology for using research materials. Chalkboard placement of the homework assignment becomes a visual notification to those present and to the occasional latecomer. If homework is made part of a handout attachment, a chalkboard reminder of its location assists youngsters in not overlooking it. Because homework is a vehicle for content continuity, the observer notes whether the instructor has successfully linked the day's lesson with the upcoming one to be taught the next day. Some instructors assign homework at the end of a lesson. This approach may appear plausible to some readers but it frequently presents problems. Should there be classroom debate near a lesson's conclusion, or an unannounced fire drill or other unexpected school events, the instructor may fail to inform the class of the homework assignment. To avoid this, it is suggested that homework notification be initiated at the introduction of an instructional period.

Lesson development. Instructional development is critical to a lesson's success. Differences in lesson development exist from teacher to teacher and lesson to lesson. The instructor initiates lesson development with a series of review questions that promote a discussion of previous content material. The teacher generally asks a series of preliminary questions based, once again, upon prior homework assignments and classroom discussion. These questions are specific in format. The supervisor is cognizant of an instructor's need to pose questions, clearly; did the teacher personalize his/her questions? During questioning, did the instructor prepare the groundwork for student socialization by permitting the arrow of recitation to flow from "teacher to student," "student to student," and then back to the teacher? Did the instructor call upon different youngsters to respond to questions or was involvement limited to one or two students?

As a teacher matures in classroom experience, he/she learns to avoid poorly phrased questions. Questions that are vague, multiple overlaid, tugging, result in poll-taking responses, or require a single "yes/no" answer, are averted. Good questions are those that are subject-specific and personalized. Frequently, these questions result in student responses that may be personalized too, but they prepare the foundation for building a lesson's superstructure. Several examples of primary or preliminary questions are:
1. "Who can review for us the characteristics and functions of the nucleus in the phylum protozoa?"
2. "Using your class notes from yesterday's lesson, can someone define for us what we mean by an 'opportunity cost?' "

      3.   "How might you describe the setting for John Stein-
          beck's *The Grapes of Wrath*?"
Preliminary questions create building blocks of factual information that serve to enforce the lesson "Aim."

    Pivotal questions are more complex and strive for a deeper
understanding of lesson content. They also provide for a greater
sustained exchange of classroom ideas. The following are examples of several thought-provoking pivotal questions that one might
observe in various subject classes:

    1."In your opinion, what physical functions make the
paramecium a unique one-celled organism?"
    2."If you were a manufacturer of a durable goods product,
what economic problems might you share with other producers
during an economic downturn of the business cycle?"
    3."Can someone describe Steinbeck's literary method for
'painting' a picture of despair in *The Grapes of Wrath*?"

    A final summary is just that! It comes at the end of the
lesson. It is introduced by a provoking question that relates to a
lesson's primary theme. Suggested conclusions are then noted, as
is with the medial summary, upon the chalkboard.

    Classroom time. The teacher should also be aware of
classroom time. A lesson is divided into teacher-determined time
frames that are completed within a class period. If this is to occur,
the teacher must be cognizant of the time devoted to each classroom function. This is not a simple task but is achieved with continued classroom exposure. Without meaning to be contradictory,
however, the experienced teacher knows that lessons are occasionally carried over. An instructor frequently confronts the dilemma
of a lesson going beyond a given class period. There are probable
causes for this to happen. An unusual number of lesson interrup-
tions by non-classroom monitors carrying school-related mes-
sages, unexpected classroom emergencies, unannounced fire and

shelter drills, and stimulating classroom discussion are only a few reasons lessons may have to be extended. The latter reason is one that the teacher has control over. At times, a decision has to be made whether to terminate a lesson in the desired time frame or to allow discussion to continue. Given a choice, it is preferable that a learning situation marked by "heated" debate be allowed to continue to the classroom bell. A "final summary" can be used as the motivational device in the next lesson being introduced, shortly thereafter, by a "sub-motivation." A supervisor observing a lesson that continues beyond the period's bell has to consider the circumstances for the teacher's decision to do so.

The teacher as a classroom leader. A teacher is a role model with a clear and pleasant speaking voice, poise, and vitality. He/she is animate and displays mastery of subject content. The AP is observant of the instructor's grasp of class management, lesson timing, democratic leadership during instruction, and rapport with individuals. When any or all such teacher characteristics are lacking, the AP informs the teacher of his/her shortfalls and suggests, when necessary, a program to remedy conditions found undesirable.

That's a "cool" idea, teacher.

Knowledge is a process of piling up facts; wisdom lies in their simplification.

Martin H. Fischer, scientist, educator

Chapter Six

The Observation Report

The written observation report. A primary aim of the written observation is the uplifting of instruction. Neither the observation nor the report is a vehicle for teacher harassment! A formal observation report is one of several reports (assuming the teacher has been observed before). Together, they serve as a history of an individual's instructional performance. The reports taken together protect the instructor from any capricious appraisal rating that may be based as a result of one negative report in particular.

The post-observation conference. After an observation, I sent a memo to the instructor requesting a meeting. Ideally, our post-conference occurred within 24-72 hours of the formal observation. The conference was often held in an empty classroom rather than the department office, so as not to be perceived by the instructor as condescending. The meeting was conducted in an informal atmosphere during the teacher's non-instructional period. A primary aim of our conference was to assist the teacher by evaluating his/her performance and when necessary to develop a "prescriptive" plan for strengthening his/her instruction. I was cordial and non-confrontational at a conference. I began the meeting with words of encouragement to the teacher. Most meetings lasted about 20 minutes. I informed the teacher of his/her lesson's strength and weaknesses. What follows are several observation opening comments, involving a variety of subjects, that might be used to began a conference.

1. Your Aim "How do we solve quadratic equations?" was clearly elicited from the class. It was restated by the teacher, placed upon the chalkboard, and read, once again, by a student volunteer.

2. There was considerable socialization, as indicated by the chain of recitation, as when you asked the well- stated question, "If you had been a member of President Roosevelt's Cabinet, in 1933, what suggestions might you have made for ending the depression?"

3. There were a good variety of student activities. Youngsters worked at their desks in small groups discussing questions raised by an excellent teacher handout related to the ecological system under study. Later in the period, students wrote answers to questions at the chalkboard. This was followed by a solid exchange of biological concepts relating to the lesson's Aim.

4. Management routines were thorough and efficiently executed. The daily attendance was taken and a homework assignment placed at the right side of the chalkboard. Class materials were distributed by student monitors in an orderly fashion indicating that they had been well trained by the teacher. The previous night's homework was collected without fanfare.

After stating lesson strengths, I would note the lesson's weaknesses. Examples of several weaknesses in no special order, follow:

1. *The lesson's motivation could not be seen (I sat in row 3, seat 7) from the far desks in most rows.*

2. *The greater part of the lesson consisted of content read from the textbook. This resulted in a lack of socialization. It wasn't until 3-4 minutes prior to the ending bell that a teacher-student discussion began. In addition, the textbook reading selection "The Physical Geography of Southeast Asia" did not relate to the lesson's Aim, "Who are the people of Southeast Asia?"*

3. *You offered a multiple question that may have created confusion in the minds of youngsters as when you asked, "what is a fulcrum?" quickly followed by, "when might someone use it?"*

4. *Chalkboard organization was weakened by brief one or double-word notations rather than short complete sentences that would express a concept or point of view. Rather than having columns headed "Plants," "Animal Cells" to demonstrate differences in physical characteristics between the two, topic headings such as "Unique Features of Plant Cells," and "Unique Features of Animal Cells" would have clarified student comprehension.*

My observations were documented and always supported by lesson citations. When citing a weakness, I offered a suggestion for correcting it. The teacher was free to interject his/her opinion at any point during the review, and I listened attentively to his/her response. If the instructor took strong exception to a criticism, I was considerate of his/her objection. There would be other opportunities, including future classroom visits that could confirm my perceived suspicions of observed instructional weakness. Visits were never delayed when I doubted a teacher's classroom effectiveness.

The written report may vary in form depending upon the writing style of the supervisor. It may also vary from one that outlines strengths, weaknesses, and suggestions to one of descriptive prose. What follows are two models for the reader to consider. The first is written in a brief style format, while the second denotes lesson specifics and teacher friendliness.

Theodore Roosevelt H.S.	Mathematics Department
David Smith, Principal	Frank Rausher, (AP, Supv.)

To: Mr. Jerry Boyd	Date of Observation: 2/4/03
Arith: Period 4-Main Building	Date of Conference: 2/13/03

Topic: Lesson on Commissions

Commendations:

    1. There was a good deal of student participation in the pacing of solutions to problems on the board. Students were periodically given the opportunity to compare their work with board solutions.

    2. The teacher gave students individual help throughout the period. Students felt free to ask for help when they needed assistance with their work.

    3. The teacher's control over the class was generally good. Most students were productively occupied for the entire period.

Suggestions:

    1. At times pupils called out answers to your questions. As we discussed at our conference, pupils should be discouraged from calling out. Try to call on non-volunteers so that all pupils may have an opportunity to contribute to the lesson.

    2. In order to assist our pupils to read and interpret problems, each lesson should contain some time devoted to the solution of narrative-type problems.

I have read and received a copy of this report:

_____   _____

Teacher   Asst. Principal (Supv.)

FR/bm
Cc: Mr. David Smith

Observation Report #1

Thomas A. Edison H.S.
Samuel Tipton, Principal
1739 Sunset Blvd.
Nice, Michigan 46386

April 14, 2003
To: Mr. Michael Phillips
From: Mr. A. Gatsby, AP Social Studies Department
RE: OBSERVATION-GLOBAL STUDIES 3,4/15/03-ROOM 234
Register: 33 Attendance: 31

Dear Michael:
Your students came into the room quietly, sat down, notebooks out, ready to work. You started the lesson by asking a series of "warm up" questions that drew upon previous material taught, noted that Martin Luther was upset by several practices of the Church—the widespread sale of indulgences, the worldliness of some of the clergy, simony, etc.
You took note of the fact that Luther's mind and soul were troubled.

Your lesson focused on the time Luther toured Germany, successfully spreading his "heresy," particularly among the German nobility. As the split between Luther and the Catholic Church widened, Luther was excommunicated when he failed to recant. The main part of your lesson centered around the Diet of Worms, a meeting convened by Charles V to ascertain if Luther was as much a political outlaw as he was a religious heretic. When he refused to retract his beliefs, the Diet declared him an outlaw. Yet, as you brought out, the princes of Germany were willing to shelter him; you noted their motives for so doing.

You developed a chalkboard chart on the feelings of each strata of German society on Martin Luther's teachings, namely, the Church, the monarch, the nobility, and the peasants. This chart provided a concise analysis of the crisis that Luther started. The actions of the Church as written on your chart follow: "1. excommunicate 2. punishment 3. considered Martin Luther the anti-Christ." (See the appended lesson plan for the complete chart as written on the chalkboard). Note: Appended lesson not included.

Observation Report #2

47

You exhibited many strengths as a teacher during this lesson. You defined orally such terms as "Diet of Worms," "infallible," "vernacular," etc. You made a valiant effort to involve all students in your lesson, at times avoiding hands that were raised, to call on students who were passive or shy. You did this throughout your lesson, even when it had the effect of slowing your lesson down. You developed your lesson logically and sequentially, starting with a good review of the previous day's work, carrying it through a series of pivotal questions ("Why in the world would the Church think a translation of the Bible into the vernacular would be dangerous?"), then analyzing Luther's stand and its effects on German society through a chalkboard chart, and, finally, ending with a summary.

You refused to accept single-word answers from your students, and you encouraged them to answer in sentences, in a sustained manner. You worked from a well-planned, detailed lesson plan. I sensed an excellent rapport between you and your Global Studies 3 students. Your chart analysis of German society was excellent. It enabled your students to understand the motives of the key players—the Church, the monarchy, the nobility, and the peasantry. Participation in your lesson was very good, and your students were motivated and interested in your discussion of theological ideas in the 16th Century, an accomplishment in itself. You took your class as far as they could go in this intellectual adventure.

Several recommendations come to mind. You did call on volunteers and non-volunteers throughout the lesson. Why not call on passive students to repeat the answers, particularly those they did not know in the first place? Have students elaborate on the answers of their peers. As you have mastered the techniques of the developmental lesson, why not, at times, experiment with this class? Using library research and cooperative learning processes, why not have the class write a playlet on the Diet of Worms? The estates of Germany would be present in the unsympathetic Diet, and Luther would be able to declare: "I cannot go against my conscience. Here I stand. I cannot do otherwise. God help me."

I'm sure that you would agree that we have to get our students away from the dull and poorly written textbook. In my opinion, the use of primary sources is the name of the game. Imagine if an English teacher had to read a two-paragraph account of Shakespeare's *Julius Caesar* instead of studying the play itself. (You told me at the post-observation conference that you intended to dramatize the Council of Trent).

This was an excellent lesson performed by an outstanding teacher.

Sincerely,

Arthur Gatsby
AP, Social Studies Department

AG/md

I have received a copy of this observation and I understand a similar copy will be placed in my file. Keep the top copy; send the other two copies back signed.

_____   _____
DATE   Michael Phillips

Evaluating the observation reports. A comparison of the two reports reveals key differences between them. The first report appears impersonal, rushed, and is an oversimplification of the observed lesson. The writer has overlooked supervisory basics; there is no indication of the arithmetic level studied, and the numerical register and attendance figures are not indicated. In addition, nine days have elapsed from the day of the observation to the post-observation conference. The "Topic," as reported by the AP, "Lesson on Commissions," raises the question as to whether this was indeed the lesson's "Aim," or was it the supervisor's perception of an "Aim"? The three commendations give the appearance of a pro forma listing of classroom events. The supervisor's "Suggestions" focus on two issues but fail to address a specific problem in detail and provide no documentation for the instructional weakness.

The second report differs from the first in its detailed description. Necessary items such as classroom identification, registration and attendance figures are indicated. The writer's salutation appears comforting and is non-hostile in tone. The opening paragraph offers a "visual" review of the lesson's beginning. The second paragraph describes the lesson's focus followed by a lesson summation. The third paragraph describes lesson development, and chalkboard work that is supported by documentation. In paragraphs four and five, the supervisor discusses teacher strengths. Paragraph six notes recommendations and indicates that discussion took place between teacher and supervisor. The report concludes positively with the AP's recognition of teacher professionalism.

First observation report considerations for a new teacher. A new teacher's first observation report impacts upon his/her self-esteem because it is perceived as an indicator of teaching success or failure. The AP understands this and seeks to allay the teacher's fear. This may be partially achieved by a written memo following a pre-observation conference but before the first formal observation. The memo describes proposed supervisory assistance with reference to a supervisor-teacher agreement regarding observation outcomes. The memo is written in a tone that motivates and instills confidence in the teacher.

John Adams High School
Frank Whitman, Principal

Inter-school Memo

To: Mrs. Blanche Smith   Date: Feb. 14, 2003
From: Mr. Bob Porter, AP, Supervision, Biology Department
Subject: Pre-Observation Conference and Proposed Plan of Assistance
Time: Period 7
Place: Room 321

Dear Blanche:

During our pre-observation conference we discussed the basic prelimi-naries for the start of a lesson. You were asked to discuss your planned approach for the lesson's implementation. We discussed the strengths and weaknesses of your lesson plan and mutually agreed to the following:

Establishing the groundwork for good class management should, at this time, be a top priority. The following suggestions were also made for your con-sideration:

a. Start by first placing a "lesson number" and the word "Aim" on the chalkboard. The actual aim will be elicited from the class during preliminary or pivotal questioning.

b. Every lesson has a motivational device. Place the motivation under the "Aim" if it is in the form of a question, quote or stick figure cartoon.

c. A homework assignment should also be placed in a convenient and routine location where it is clearly seen by students.

d. After taking attendance, collect previous homework and note stu-dents who have willingly failed to do it in your class record book. Inform the class of important announcements.

I informed you that I would be interested in observing the implementa-tion of these particulars primarily and that additional assistance would be forth-coming for other teaching components, such as:

Page 2-Mrs. Blanche Smith, Pre-observation Conference

    a. questioning technique
    b. lesson development
    c. adequate use of materials
    d. chalkboard organization and summaries

    You noted that my suggestions were "helpful" and that you understood the need for good classroom management.
    You are a conscientious individual. You show interest in your students and demonstrate promise as a teaching professional.

        Respectfully,

        Robert Porter
        Assistant Principal, Supervision
        Department of Biology

I have read this report and understand that a copy will be placed in my file. I also understand that I have the right of rebuttal.

_____

Teacher Signature: Blanche Smith

    The next three reports reflect supervisory continuity in providing instructional guidance to a novice teacher. They are offered to demonstrate the role of AP reports in a teacher's professional development.

Pre-Observation Memo #1

September 16, 2003

To: Ms. Susan Donner
From: Bert Halprin, AP (SUPV.) Social Studies Dept.
Subject: Pre-Observation Conference and Proposed Plan of Assistance
Time: Period 7
Place: Room 417

Dear Susan:

During our meeting of 9/14/03, we discussed the preliminaries for the beginning of a lesson. You were asked to discuss your present approach and whether you thought there was a need to change any procedural steps. A discussion of procedural strengths and weaknesses followed.

It was mutually agreed upon that an organized and planned approach was necessary to improve lesson timing and development. The following steps were suggested for launching the lesson:

a- Begin a lesson by placing a lesson identifier, such as a number, in the upper right corner of the chalkboard, followed by the word "Aim."
b- Every lesson has a motivational device. The motivation could be placed under the word "Aim' in the form of a "warmup" question, a stick figure cartoon, appropriate visuals along the board ledge, such as photographs, illustrations, or objects that pertain to the lesson's theme.
c- A homework assignment should also be placed on the board at a convenient and routine location. The homework should be numbered, to show continuity, and the assignment clearly defined as to the task to be completed by students. Attendance taking should follow.
d- After taking attendance, the previous night's homework should be collected, 'a rotational system' was previously suggested, and students with no homework should be quickly noted in the teacher's record book. School and/or teacher announcements follow.

53

Page 2-Ms. Susan Donner

You were informed that during your first formal observation, mutually scheduled for Thursday, October 1, 2003, period 9, Global Studies 1 class, that the Chair would be particularly interested in observing the implementation of the afore-mentioned suggestions. Additional assistance would be forthcoming with regard to the following:

        a- questioning technique
        b- lesson development
        c- adequate use of materials
        d- chalkboard organization

You remarked that you thought that my suggestions "were meaningful and help-ful" and agreed to make an effort to implement them during the upcoming obser-vation.

Susan, you are a conscientious teaching novice who shows enthusiasm and a desire to succeed. Most positive is your willingness to accept criticism and the desire to grow in professional stature.

                    Respectfully,

                    Bert
                    Bert Halprin
                    Assistant Principal, Supv.
                    Social Studies

I have read this report and understand that a copy will be placed in my file. I also understand that I have the right of rebuttal. _____ Initials

Observation Report #1

To: Ms. Susan Donnor
From: Bert Halprin, AP (SUPV.) Social Studies Dept.
Observation of October 1, 2003, Global Studies 1
Class Attendance: 2 of 34 absent, Period 9, Rm. 416
Post-Observation Conference: October 3, 2003

October 5, 2003

Dear Susan:

It was most positive to note that you have implemented many of the suggestions we spoke about during our pre-observation conference of September 23, 2003.

You began your class in an orderly and professional manner. You entered the room, placed a numerical lesson identifier, the word "Aim," which eventually was elicited from your class as "How Have Middle Eastern Cities Developed?" and an appropriate homework assignment on the chalkboard. Beneath the word "Aim" you placed a motivational device that consisted of two stick figures "discussing" urban issues in the Middle East.

Your opening question, "Why do some people think that going to a city might make them wealthy?" began class debate as noted by the enthusiastic response of your students. You attempted to structure these responses upon the chalkboard under the heading "Cities." As a result of this activity you were able to successfully elicit, write, and define the terms *economic, political, and culture*.

Might I offer a few suggestions that we discussed at our post-observation conference of 10/3/03? Stress to your students that they are not to linger about the room after entering the class, but that they should immediately take their seats and begin to copy notes from the chalkboard. Several students, apparently, were unaware of your procedure for the beginning of a lesson.

Page 2-Ms. Susan Donner

I think your chalkboard header "Cities" was a bit vague, and that the rephrasing of the topic question to, "What Have Been the Contributions of 'The City' to Society?" might have been more self-explanatory in terms of what you were actually trying to stress.

Several of your questions were quite good and stirred student interest, as when you asked, "How would you define a city?" and "What factors, in your opinion, make a city an economic center?" Such personalized questions were thought provoking and led to an excellent response. There were several question types that should be avoided, particularly those whose answers led to a "yes" or "no" response. Your question "Do you think people perceive cities as being centers of power?" might have been better served as "In what ways do you perceive cities as being centers of people power?" In addition, try to avoid "tugging" questions, as when you asked, "The political center of a city involves what people?" Such a question might have been better phrased as, "Can you name several types of agencies or departments that might be necessary for operating a city more efficiently?"

Susan, you certainly are off to a good start. Please see me during a free period on or about Wednesday, 10/8/03 to arrange for another instructional tutorial. At that time, we will also discuss student absenteeism in your period 1 Global Studies class and what might be done do to improve the situation. Keep up the solid effort!

Sincerely,

Bert
Bert Halprin
Assistant Principal (SUPV.)
Social Studies Department

I have read and received a copy of this report and understand it will be placed in my file. I know that I have the right of rebuttal.

_____
Teacher Signature

Post Observation Memo #1

October 14, 2003

To: Ms. Susan Donner
From: Bert Halprin, AP (SUPV.) Social Studies Dept.
Post Observation Assistance, October 8, 2003
Period 7
Room: 417

Dear Susan:

At our third meeting of October 8, 2003, you informed me that you found my previous suggestions for "beginning the lesson" to be very helpful. I was happy to learn that you were comfortable using my suggested approach and that you were making progress with your instruction.

At our meeting we spoke about the poor attendance situation in your period 1 Global Studies class. You informed me that of 28 students on register, you have filed 14 lateness or cutting cards with the Attendance Office. I indicated that you should note the dates of the filings in your marking book should parental or school inquiries be made in the near future. It was further suggested that you make home phone calls and/or mail Department warning letters to student homes to alert parents of the situation. You informed me that you have already begun this process.

We next turned our attention to the continuing discussion of classroom management and lesson development. A chief concern of yours was how to best curtail use of the classroom "pass." You indicated that you were having somewhat of a problem with this. I suggested that you make it generally known that the pass was "to be used but not abused." To accomplish this, you might denote a specific number of times for use of the pass per period.

Page 2-Ms. Susan Donner

Further, stress that those continually asking for the pass bring a note from a doctor explaining their frequent need to leave the room. It is important that you control this situation! Be sure to have those that leave the room sign a daily sheet for pass use. This record can be used as a reference should a parent request proof of a school violation brought against a student while out of your room. Save the "pass use" sheet for a term.

Time was also spent discussing questioning technique. You informed me that you remembered not to ask "tugging" questions or those requiring only a "yes" or "no" answer. I recommended that your lesson plan include questions that relate to your students' personal experiences. This is best achieved by the use of personal pronouns such as "you," "we," and "our." For example, in your previous lesson on Middle Eastern cities, you might have asked, "How might you have felt had your family moved from a desert environment to a large city?" instead of "What is it like to move from the desert to the city?" Had you been discussing, in your World History 2 class, Napoleon's expansion into Russia in 1812, you might ask a question following a short narrative. For example, "In hope of teaching the Russians a lesson for breaking the Continental System instituted by France, Napoleon decided to invade Russia. Had you been a member of Napoleon's military council, why might you have suggested that an invasion of Russia not take place?"

This technique serves dual purposes:

a) it provides a review of events previously discussed.
b) it relates historical material in a way that involves active student participation.

Our attention also turned to making adequate use of the chalkboard for outlining student and teacher responses under topic headings. It was suggested that short sentences be used rather than single word notations. This assists students to recall complete thoughts rather than several detached words. It also assists students to organize their thoughts when reviewing notebook materials.

Page 3-Ms. Susan Donner

In conclusion, I asked that you visit Mr. Peter Rayburn's class during the week of October 18, 2003, to observe his economics class. I indicated that I would make arrangements for this. The purpose of this visit is to observe the following:

a) How is the lesson launched?
b) What are the strengths and weaknesses in his questioning technique?
c) What are the strengths and weaknesses in his use of the chalkboard?

Our next meeting will follow after your observation of Mr. Rayburn's lesson. Memo to follow indicating time, period, and place for our visit.

Respectfully,

Bert
Bert Halprin
Assist. Principal (SUPV.)
Social Studies Department

I have read and received a copy of this memo and am aware that a copy will be placed in my file. (Please sign and return one of the two copies.)

_____
Teacher Signature

Stimulating students to think!

Every truth passes through three stages before it is recognized. In the first, it is ridiculed; in the second, it is opposed; in the third, it is regarded as self-evident.

Arthur Schopenhauer, philosopher

Chapter Seven

Demonstration Workshops and Inter-Department Visitations

The demonstration workshop and inter-department visit. Demonstration workshops and inter-department visits are vehicles for instructional improvement. They offer shared group experiences and permit teacher feedback. A well-planned demonstration workshop offers teachers fundamental appreciation for what can be achieved in the classroom. Ideally, a planned demonstration is inclusive of all department members, not just a select group. One problem, always present, is the time restraint placed upon both teachers and students when a workshop is held during an instructional day.

When I first began my initial teacher observations, I witnessed conspicuous instructional weaknesses among staff members. I decided there was a need for a series of teacher workshops. What I failed to anticipate were the numerous problems such an undertaking entails. I wanted all staff members present at a workshop. I also felt that student participation would alleviate teacher perceptions that a workshop was pro forma. Similarly, if students did participate, I had to decide whether I needed "average" academic youngsters or a special group of students. Another consideration was whether to schedule this conference during regular school hours or during a student non-attendance day. There were other concerns, too. Should I, or should a staff member, lead the workshop, one who was willing and competent to do so. I had to consider the physical space needed and its availability. A logistics dilemma was in securing teacher coverage to replace those attending the workshop.

Identifying instructional problems is achieved by assessment. Demonstration workshops should focus on topics that offer immediate teaching benefit to most teachers. No single workshop will improve teaching skills entirely. Prior to a workshop, teaching observers are provided copies of the demonstration's lesson plan along with any student printouts. In addition, the supervisor provides each observer with a guide sheet for lesson evaluation. A model guide sheet follows:

A Teacher's Evaluation Guide for Demonstrations and Inter-Department Visitations

A. The Lesson

1. Preliminaries:
    a. Is there an "Aim"? Is it appropriate to the lesson and to student needs?
    b. Is the "Aim" clearly stated by students? The teacher?
    c. Is it legibly written on the chalkboard and positioned for all to see?
    d. Is homework assigned? Is it motivated? How was this accomplished?
    e. Is there a motivational device? Does it reflect the lesson "Aim"? In what way?

2. Teacher Planning:
    a. Does the lesson demonstrate continuity? In what way?
    b. Is the level of difficulty appropriate for the students?
    c. Does the lesson components appear to have planned time sequences?
    d. Are students given an opportunity for self-expression? How so?
    e. Are there medial and final summaries?

3. Materials:
    a. Does the instructor make adequate use of the chalkboard? Has it been effectively used? Explain.
    b. Is there use of audio-visual materials, textbooks, or illustrative materials? How have they been made part of the lesson? Have they been effective? In what ways?

4. Questioning technique:
   a. How does the instructor phrase questions? Are they thought provoking? Explain.
   b. Are questions introduced with pronouns so that they meet student needs? Examples?
   c. Do questions produce discussion as noted by an "arrow of recitation"?
   d. Are questions clearly stated, or are some questions vague or "spoon-fed"? Do questions require only a "yes" or "no" response; are any multi-faceted or direct and to the point? Examples of any type.

B. The Students
   1. Activities:
      a. Is there socialization? Is the instructor a facilitator or a dominator of the lesson? How is this made apparent?
      b. Are youngsters engaged in a variety of classroom activities? How have they been initiated? How successful?
      c. Is student interest maintained by adjustments to individualized abilities when necessary? How is it done?
      d. Is student to teacher and student to student interaction harmonious? In what ways are they demonstrable?
      e. Are student experiences enhanced by working in groups, pairs, or committees? Is there opportunity for special abilities and interests? Examples.

2. Outcomes:
    a. Did student participation assist in achieving the lesson's "Aim"? To what extent?
    b. Was the lesson an accomplished one? Have student skills been enhanced? Have specific outcomes been achieved?
    c. Were student interests and imaginations stimulated? How was this done?

C. Teacher
    a. Is the teacher adequately prepared? Explain.
    b. Does the teacher exhibit positive qualities of voice and English usage?
    c. Does the instructor demonstrate command of administrative classroom routines? Describe briefly.
    d. Does the teacher demonstrate grasp of his/her subject matter? What makes you think so?
    e. Is the teacher alert to classroom activities? Examples?
    f. Does he/she demonstrate assistance and guidance to students? How?

A time frame for evaluating any conference has to be considered; should it occur during a phase of the workshop or at a later date? During the evaluation phase, the Chair guides discussion and helps teachers to narrow in upon specific areas of instruction.

The Assistant Principal at the helm!

With every deed you are sowing a seed, though the harvest you may not see.

Ella Wheeler Wilcox, poet

Chapter Eight

Establishing Department Homework Policy

Student study skills. Experience indicates that most youngsters entering high school lack solid study skills. In that different subjects demonstrate a requisite for specific study techniques, it is vital that high school teachers assume the responsibility for providing study guidance for their students. Students need to develop efficient study skills, acquire responsibility for learning, and adapt themselves to new tools of inquiry for a technological age. Instruction in "how to study" requires repetitive application, especially for those youngsters who are "freshmen." Ninth graders should be taught how to plan their study time. They should be assisted in achieving skills for critical reading, reviewing content materials, evaluating and analyzing problems, using the library for research, note taking, acquiring an expanded vocabulary, and interpreting graphs and charts.

During our first department conference of a new term, teachers were reminded to set aside class time, from content instruction, to provide students with study assistance. I alerted my staff to emphasize student study skills by integrating "how to study" techniques into classroom and homework assignments. Teachers were asked to note homework as an important vehicle for strengthening student study habits, work routines, and written expression. Early in a term, teachers set aside two or three periods for "How might I develop good study habits?" lessons. Youngsters previously exposed to similar lessons gained a benefit from reinforcement. My staff demonstrated the creation and use of a daily/weekly after-school schedule, including time frames, for student work and study. This was particularly useful for those youngsters working part time. Instructors also discussed, with their classes, the merits of a quiet study place, the need for adequate lighting, and for a desk/table and a comfortable chair. Once study basics were explained and then discussed, the teacher initiated instruction for uplifting reading and writing skills.

Uniform homework preparation. This writer is an advocate of uniform homework in all subject areas. Creation of these assignments is undertaken with the cooperation of the department's staff. Under my direction, each subject teacher was assigned a portion of his/her course content. Using copies of course texts and the mandated curriculum for a subject area, the teacher pre-read portions of the text and created a series of questions that students would answer for homework. I requested that each teacher prepare a specific number of homework assignments for the subject content he/she had been assigned. Upon their completion, the assignment questions were integrated beneath course topics and reviewed by a committee of teachers for inconsistencies, clarity, level of difficulty, and English usage. Once reviewed, assignments were finalized in preparation for typing/printing under my supervision. The uniform homework assignments were evaluated every two years for needed modification or when a class text was replaced with another one.

Although some teachers might advocate preparing their own homework assignments, pre-written assignments have advantages that outweigh preconceived disadvantages. In that they are developed and monitored by a group of teachers improves the possibility that assignments not lack clarity or be overly demanding. Uniform assignments make students aware of their term responsibilities while permitting them to plan ahead to meet course requirements. In addition, they provide absentee youngsters, and those transferring from another same subject classroom, with a continued link to subject content and sequence.

Uniform homework assignments are not the absolute they may appear to be. The classroom teacher has flexibility in modifying or delaying an assignment at any time. All that is necessary is for the teacher to inform his/her class that a "uniform homework assignment is being delayed and a new one is to be completed instead of #26 [an example], from the uniform homework sheets." The instructor motivates the new assignment after writing it on the chalkboard at an appropriate location. A finalized set of uniform homework sheets should provide students with a directional opening paragraph of instructions. It might appear as follows:

AMERICAN HISTORY 2: UNIFORM HOMEWORK SHEETS

Students are to use the "Aims," pivotal questions and homework assignments for each lesson. These questions contain specific knowledge, understandings and skills needed to master the lesson. Students are required to answer questions in their homework subject section. They are also expected to demonstrate subject mastery to these questions during the classroom lesson. If a student is absent, he/she is expected to continue with the assignments until his/her return to the subject class. The student need not rewrite the questions. Cut off each given homework assignment with a scissor and scotch tape it to the homework paper. Then, in well-written prose, write your answers below the questions.

Note: Replacement of lost homework sheets will not be provided by the subject teacher. Copies will have to be made from those of classmates. Keep sheets in a safe place at home for your use. All readings and assignments have been keyed to the text,

<u>American History</u>, Bellows and Long, Stone Book Publishers, Inc., 2003.

Beneath the directions begins the first of a number of continuing homework assignments. The reader will note that each assignment has a homework number, assigned pages, an Aim and the questions to be answered. Assignments are created with the intent of not overloading youngsters. Each night's homework should take, typically, no longer than forty minutes to one hour to complete. A typical assignment format might appear as follows:

#1 Was the United States justified in going to war with Spain in 1898?
(Pages 439-445)

1) Why were the Cuban people dissatisfied with Spanish rule?
2) In your opinion, why was there American interest in Cuba?
3) What role did the "yellow press" play in arousing American sympathies for the Cuban people?
4) Had you been alive in 1898, what impact might the "de Lome letter" and the sinking of the Maine have had on you?
5) List <u>three</u> major results of the Spanish-American War.
6) How would you describe the relationship between Cuba and the United States immediately after the War?

Uniform homework assignments guide students through much factual information and narrow in upon specifics vital to subject development and understanding. The teacher is not limited solely to this type of assignment. Homework could have questions requiring interpretation of textual material that culminate in the writing of essays. In addition, there could be a variety of assignments involving the preparation of maps, statistical information, or other forms of visual data. Such decisions are left to the discretion of the individual classroom teacher.

The cart before the horse is neither beautiful nor useful.

Henry David Thoreau, author

Chapter Nine

Student Testing

Student testing. A department's testing policy is designed to evaluate student achievement, discover individual abilities, and to appraise the progress of slow, average, exceptional, and handicapped learners. It is additionally designed to assist youngsters in motivating them to achieve academic goals. Testing policy relates, similarly, to teachers. It is used to evaluate teacher effectiveness, their procedures, classroom materials, and to measure the reliability of instructional innovations. Test policy also provides a systematic basis for student classification, acceleration, and promotion and permits the supplementary reporting of an individual's progress to parents. It assists guidance personnel with timely student academic updates.

In a speech before the Los Angeles World Affair Council, U.S. Secretary of Education, Rod Paige stated that,

Accountability means making sure no child is left behind by keeping track of every child's progress...accountability requires specific, objective data...test scores give us the information we need to find out what works, find out who needs help, and to give more information and control to the people closet to the action: the parents, teachers, administrators and the communities.[2]

Secretary Paige's remarks addresses objective test data for determining student progress in meeting state standards derived by statewide assessment. It should be noted that federal law does not discourage testing in subject areas, in addition to reading and mathematics, for determining student achievement. Departmental tests, measured by assessment indicators developed by the AP and the instructional staff jointly, could be reliable indicators of student progress in a subject area while increasing the probability of youngsters not "falling through the cracks" in the pursuit of a meaningful high school diploma.

The AP understands that testing plays an important role in achieving school objectives. When I first undertook my duties, I perceived that many teachers lacked an appreciation for "testing." I therefore familiarized my staff with test intent, its design. and administration. This was especially important during the orientation of novice teachers. In addition to my daily tasks, department preparation for standardized exams was a test of my endurance. Preparation for standardized exams began long before the day of the test. Teachers and students had to be notified of the upcoming test in advance, with the time, place, and necessary requirements for administering the exam.

In many large urban schools, a standardized test day often results in the school population being placed on a new, but temporary, program footing. In addition to needing teacher proctors for

---

[2] *Secretary Paige Unveils New Testing Guide for Families, Schools and Communities*, 13 February, 2002, U.S. Department of Education Press Release

specific assignments, standby instructors are necessary for emergencies. I was responsible for the dispersal of test materials to the teacher proctors. Packets of test booklets, test answer sheets, scrap paper, pencils, and a list of scheduled student test takers had to be placed into large envelopes and labeled with the assigned proctor's name and room number. My job did not stop there. Upon completion of an exam, a "return of exam" routine had to be in place so that proctors returned test contents to a predetermined site that permitted me necessary control and security of the completed test.

Constructing a good test. The subject test is an important component of the learning environment. It is by no means a total measure of what a student has learned. It is, however, an indicator of a youngster's progress in learning subject content. It is vital that teachers' understand the necessity for good test design and that a test measure what it is intended to measure! A good test is an indicator of what students have or have not learned, and assists the instructor in discovering unit objectives that were, or were not, achieved. A good test is reliable (two instructors would assign the same score to the same response) and consistent in its objective. It is clearly defined in its intent; are test items, for example, diagnostic, revealing student strengths and weaknesses, or are they designed primarily to evaluate individual achievement and a youngster's ranking of content mastery?

A good test emphasizes what has been taught in class. It does not penalize youngsters who work slowly or those that may have reading disabilities. Test design does not place priority on rote memorization, unimportant details, or ambiguous questions. A good test uses a variety of items to enlarge the range of measurement and provides for "straightforwardness" in administering and interpreting results. There are a variety of test formats the teacher can use as a basis for achieving good test design. Some, but not all, follow:

1. The multiple-choice test
2. The true-false test
3. The matching test
4. The completion or fill-in test
5. The essay test
6. The oral presentation test
7. The case study test

In addition, the teacher has the choice of site selection for administering a test. More about this option shortly.

The multiple-choice, true-false, and completion tests are all objective exam formats. As such, they all offer advantages as well as problems. Their positive features are that exam answers are either right or wrong and are easy to mark. The problems they pose are more complex. When these formats are used, the teacher can easily offer an uneven sampling of test items which in turn produce an unequal weighing for the exam. Further, a case can be made for the argument that inadequate critical thinking occurs when answering objective test items; that emphasis rests primarily upon the student's ability to memorize content material. Other test formats, previously listed, are subjective types. These, although having theoretical limitations of their own, are more advantageous than objective tests. They call upon students to demonstrate acquired multiple skills, thereby enabling them to be more critical in their thinking.

The oral presentation test is undertaken when the teacher desires to communicate information to others. It examines a youngster's grasp of cause-effect relationships and then presents his/her conclusions before the class and the instructor.

The case study, or discovery test, asks the student to investigate something unfamiliar. For example, the teacher might direct classroom members to a local museum. Students are provided with a set of teacher-directed questions to be answered when viewing a particular exhibit related to class study. Youngsters are required, at a later date, to evaluate their findings either orally or written.

The teacher sets learning goals for both the individual student and the class as a whole. He/she tests to measure individual achievement and class success. The test becomes an indicator of the progress made. Many teachers initiate testing procedures of habit. Their routine consists of announcing an exam several days before it is administered. The class is informed of the lessons and test pages to study. On "test day" the youngsters are administered the exam that they complete within a specified time frame.

The teacher should consider alternating both the test routine and the test site. The majority of teachers do not quiz frequently enough. As a result, students are required to spend considerable time in rote memorization of notes and homework in preparation for test day. For many young people this is often a difficult task tending to favor those with retention ability and no learning disabilities while handicapping others who may be less academically inclined. Generally, rote-memorization of notes is a hindrance to critical thinking in preparation for a test.

Alternative testing methods. My experiences dictate that there are other methods for conducting class tests. For example, at the end of the school week, I gave students a short subjective quiz that covered the week's classroom content and homework. These quizzes were altered in style. On one occasion I might give a written multiple-choice, true-false, or fill-in test consisting of ten questions to be completed in seven or eight minutes. On another occasion I would read questions aloud to the class, and students recorded their answers upon pre-distributed blank quiz papers. I informed my students that each question would be read twice and that they should listen attentively before writing their answers next to the appropriate question number. This format called upon youngsters to acquire good listening habits so that they could adapt to oral questioning in the future. After administering an oral quiz, I would pause for 15-20 seconds so that the youngsters could review their answers. Once completed, the quiz was graded, in-class, by the students.

Students grading tests. Youngsters love to grade papers. They also wish to know their test grades, quickly. Having the class grade a quiz serves a dual purpose with the bonus that the teacher is "rescued" from the task of grading twenty-five to thirty short quiz papers. Although this method for scoring short individual tests curtails grading privacy, the positive feature is that youngsters are involved in a function that is important to them. In addition, the very process of grading in this manner offers the class the benefit of a post-exam review of content material. To foster democracy in the classroom, I offered this method for grading papers to a class vote early in a term. Class decision was binding upon all class members. It was I, however, who decided whether positives outweighed negatives in having the class grade a short quiz.

After I announced that the quiz was over, put down all pens, the last student in each row stood and brought his/her test paper to the person sitting in the first seat of their row, placed it upon that desk and then returned to his/her seat, while the others passed their papers back one seat. Each student was asked to sign his/her name at the bottom of the test paper. He/she became an official grader and was responsible for correctly marking the quiz. Students were informed that if there were any unusual or unexplained discrepancies in a student's quiz grade upon the return of the papers, one or two points would be deducted from the student who graded the quiz.

I then proceeded to give grading instruction to the class. I would say, "I will read each question, which will be followed by student responses to the question. If I state that an answer is correct, you will place no mark on the paper. If an answer is incorrect, you will place an X next to the appropriate number. If there are blank spaces next to a question number, you are to place a circle with a line through it and then place an X next to its corresponding number." I then read each quiz question and class members offered answers. When grading was completed, I informed the class that each correct answer had a value of one point. They were to place a correct score neatly at the top of the paper with a circle around it. Papers were quickly collected. Any student receiving a grade of six or higher was verbally informed of it by my reading the score aloud. A failing score was read only if a youngster requested it. I recorded the test scores at a later time into my grading book and returned the quizzes, usually, by the next class meeting. This entire procedure usually took no longer than twenty minutes. For the remainder of the class period, a previous lesson was finished, if left undone, or I initiated a new one.

Changing the essay test format. A full-period test can also be altered in style to meet student needs. Assume a subject teacher desires to offer an essay exam during a typical forty-minute period. He/she has completed a particular unit of study and now wishes to subjectively test the youngsters. The teacher desires to know if students have mastered unit concepts and if they can describe acquired information in an organized and documented manner.

The teacher prepares a class test sheet with two or three essays that is distributed to students approximately one week before an in-class exam. At the top of these papers are teacher directions to be followed. Essay test questions are brief and clear in meaning. The instructor distributes a test sheet to each student. Youngsters are informed that they may prepare their essays at home using their text, class notes, and other resources to help them write their first few drafts and final copy. Students are informed that essay answers should be well organized, events, names and dates clearly defined, and the written work carefully checked for English usage. When this has been done, and they are satisfied with their work, they are to put their final copy answers to memory. In a week's time they are given an opportunity to recreate their essay answers, from memory, in class. Students are pre-informed that the teacher will select either one of two or one of three essays to answer the day of the exam.

This same process can be pursued for a variety of essay tests. In addition, the teacher has the choice of giving a take-home essay exam without testing in class. In this scenario, a student draft is first submitted to the teacher. The draft is teacher reviewed, with his/her indicated recommendations, and returned to the youngster. The student's final copy is resubmitted, at a specified date, for a grade. A take-home test model in which the teacher assists youngsters in finding information for completing an exam follows:

Biology II
John Smith, Teacher
Test #3

This is a take-home exam once again. However, this time you do not have to memorize your essay answers. You should first prepare an outline answer to all three parts below and then combine them into one unified essay. Your test will be graded for both content and English usage. This exam is due no later than May 12, 2003. I have given you some assistance by numbering the pages in your textbook where you can find additional information to supplement classroom notes.

A. State Jean-Baptiste de Lamarck's Theory of Evolution. (262-64)

B. Discuss how 19th century biologists prepared the way for our understanding of evolutionary change. Be sure to discuss the contributions of the following: (270-72)

1. August Weismann
2. Charles Darwin

C. How did genetic principles discovered in the 20th century modify Darwin's theory of natural selection? (286-88)

Often to lose patience is to lose the battle.

Mohandas Gandhi, Indian nationalist leader

Chapter Ten

Guidance and Discipline

The AP's role in school guidance. The school's guidance program plays an important role in the psychological and physical development of young people. Guidance is intrinsic in every high school subject. In the social studies, for example, a youngster learns the meaning of citizenship and of the diverse social relationships in an interdependent world. In the language arts, a student learns the processes of reading, writing, and oral expression. In music and art, guidance enhances the development of individual talent and expression. Education is guidance! It prepares one for living in society.

The guidance counselor advocates the psychological stability of every student, and helping each to discover a variety of options for resolving personal dilemmas. Most teachers agree with this vision long-term, but differ with it in the short term. On a daily basis, the teacher's immediate concerns are for group well-being, good classroom behavior, and positive instructional activities. The supervisor's perception of guidance rests in reconciling the former points of view into a synthesis that places priority on common educational goals, a resolution to school conflicts that impact the student population, and in clarifying distinctions between discipline and guidance.

Articulation with the grade school. In most urban areas, the high school recruits "freshmen" from middle and junior high schools. To do this the high school frequently sends an articulation team of administrators, guidance personnel, and teachers each spring to visit local schools in its recruiting effort. The team, in conjunction with the guidance staff of the visited school, arranges an auditorium program for graduating pupils whose goal is to disseminate information pertaining to the high school's academic and vocational offerings, its unique features, special services, and requirements for admission.

As a member of our school's articulation committee, I needed to secure necessary academic information of incoming students; how many students planned to file admission applications, what were their aptitudes, abilities, and special needs. Gathering this information was necessary for proper placement of these youngsters into subject classes. This information also helped me in evaluating our course offerings, tracking options, and special programming needs.

Prior to the start of a new academic year, I participated with our school administration in a special program for incoming students and their guardians. At the orientation program, incoming youngsters and family members were informed of course offerings, need-based programs, school-wide standards, and of the criteria used in appraising student achievement. When necessary, I scheduled appointments with family members to discuss personal concerns about educational matters.

Other guidance-specific responsibilities included my tracking juniors and seniors in meeting their graduation requirements. Students on the verge of not graduating were informed of the need to repeat subject failures in night or summer school. Opportunity was afforded youngsters with strong academic performance to register for advance-placement courses. Guidance and department offices carefully tracked all these students. I provided additional guidance services by organizing school-wide cultural event presentations. These often involved communicating with a host of community speakers. Prior to an Election Day, I arranged, with assistance from the local Board of Elections, for the loan of a voting booth. The booth became the focus of a mock voting program involving students and community issues. The Election Day program always proved to be a positive vehicle for stimulating enthusiasm and civic responsibility. I also assisted in organizing school trips, book fairs, and school clubs, while the needs of the senior class involved my being a liaison to the community, colleges, and universities across the nation.

Classroom guidance and discipline. Discipline is a prerequisite for instruction. If instruction is to be successful, the teacher must establish order-producing routines. The instructor who enhances student self-discipline by means of his/her mutual cooperation and rapport increases the potential for positive learning outcomes. These outcomes are most achievable when students view school activities as rewarding.

Discipline is a characteristic of guidance. The caring teacher who establishes an affable classroom atmosphere identifiable by attributes of courtesy, concern, security, and cooperation, motivates student self-control and responsibility. Teachers whose classroom management rests on a foundation of preventive discipline (see Chapter Four) are more than likely to achieve instructional success. There is no guarantee, however, that classrooms will always be free of discipline problems.

Most discipline infractions are the result of adolescent "growing pains," hyped-up energy, having a "bad day," or some negative response to a particular classroom condition or event. Frequently, all that is necessary is the teacher's stern command to "change your seat" or "please keep quiet" to allay a problem from getting out of hand. Students, however, who frequently misbehave may be more symptomatic of a personal or social maladjustment. A case in point!

One day, early in a new term, I received an urgent memo from a veteran teacher. She had written to me about a 15-year-old boy who constantly interrupted her class. She was at "her wits end" in trying to get him to cooperate. He wouldn't. The teacher had written me the boy's name, a brief background description, and the seat and row he occupied in her class. The next day, about fifteen minutes into the teacher's lesson, I inconspicuously peered through the paned window of the classroom door and observed the youngster in question placing his legs upon his desktop and leaning back in his seat with hands behind his head. I saw his lips moving. The teacher stopped her lesson. I knocked gently upon the door, asked to see the boy, and escorted him to my office. Upon questioning his behavior and receiving no response, I called his home.

The next day I met with both the mother and son. During our conversation, the mother hesitatingly revealed that her son had a "handicap," but that she had not informed the schools of it. Somehow the lower schools failed to identify a problem. I suggested to the mother that her son undergo an evaluation. The mother became fearful. I did manage to convince her it was in her son's best interest and well-being that the family have a professional assessment of his situation. About a week later, the Guidance Office informed me that the student in question was in need of special services and would be transferred to a more suitable school environment. Situations like this shouldn't happen, but regrettably they do, occasionally.

The classroom teacher needs to acquire an awareness of differences in student behavior. Repetition of discipline infractions are usually indicative of a guidance problem that must be dealt with. The AP has a role to play in preparing his/her staff to recognize these students who demonstrate a need for special guidance assistance. How does the Assistant Principal determine the status of classroom discipline within his/her department? In Chapter Four, the role of the supervisor in affecting preventive discipline measures was discussed.

The AP assesses discipline in his/her own classes as well as in those of others by observation and monitoring teacher assistance requests. Good class management and lesson planning limit the causes of misbehavior. Teachers who forward excessive discipline referrals, or instructors who have discipline problems but transmit few or no referrals, frequently lack an understanding of the cause-effect relationships of classroom dilemmas. In these instances, the Chair assists teachers to instill management routines that limit discipline problems.

A vital school component!

Criticism should not be querulous and wasting, all knife and root-puller, but guiding, instructive, inspiring.

Ralph Waldo Emerson, author

Chapter Eleven

Scheduling Students and Teachers

Programming considerations. Skillful programming assists the school in achieving instructional objectives by providing guidance services, establishing inter-school relationships, initiating department and student activities, permitting optimum use of the teaching staff and strengthening school morale. The essential outcome of adroit programming is effective school functioning!

Numerous human factors, the curricula, State/local mandates and space availability all impact the school program. One cannot program a school without first knowing the total student population enrollment and the number of instructors needed. Schools with a "fluid" student population that results in substantial absenteeism and/or turnover rate, or one with a large percentage of non-English speaking youngsters, frequently present programming obstacles. To such a mix may be added students who are on special academic/vocational tracks, and those who have completed make-up courses in night/summer school and are in need of a readjustment of classes. In many localities throughout the nation, Teacher Union-Board of Education contract requirements pose an additional ingredient of the programming dilemma.

In many urban high schools, the AP works with the Program Committee, guidance staff and the school principal to achieve specific programming needs. Initially, the AP informs the Program Committee of a department's preliminary programming needs for the new term. The Chair determines the number of class offerings for remedial, regular, and honor courses. Second, elective courses if any, are proposed to the Committee. When approved, students who have made prior written requests through the department office, or who have been recommended by Guidance for an elective, are programmed before the start of the new term. In some instances, there may be a need to adjust or "fine tune" student programs resulting from unexpected individual problems. Such events can impede a smooth opening at the start of a term.

In school districts bound by Union accords, the AP considers contract provisions when scheduling teachers. Contract provisions vary, from locale to locale, and frequently concern building or administrative assignments, teaching rotation, the maximum allowable number of teaching periods and/or consecutive instructional periods, limits upon the number of teaching preparations, and students per class. In high schools with large student populations there is often a need to have two, or three overlapping school sessions (early and late) encompassing the main building and at times a supportive annex. This, too, can complicate programming.

Each term I considered "teacher factors" before programming. Prior to the start of a term, I requested my staff to complete a prepared form that I placed into mailboxes, indicating their subject and session preferences. The work schedule was especially burdensome for working "teacher-mothers" in the department when the school was on multi-sessions, and I took this into consideration. My attempts to assist teachers was appreciated by most and served as a quid pro quo when department approval was needed for some special project.

It is difficult to honor all teacher scheduling requests when a host of variables are linked to the programming equation. Teachers with non-teaching assignments are usually programmed with fewer teaching classes, thus creating a need to realign instructional periods. Similarly, in the case of novice instructors, it is desirable they be programmed with a common free period, when feasible, for individual or group meetings. It is important for teacher morale to rotate preferable assignments, provide subject and room location preferences to those with "traveling" programs, and maintain the number of preparations to a minimum. Programming variables are many! In fairness to staff, these factors must be reconsidered each new term.

At the heart of programming is the AP's concern for the youngsters. Establishing sound department relationships helps to facilitate the programming process. Harmony is achieved when one creates a climate of mutual support and respect between the AP and teachers. A teaching AP also demonstrates his/her willingness to assume difficult class assignments and to act as a "buddy" to novice teachers during their period of adjustment. The programming process is a common department endeavor undertaken in an atmosphere of fairness to instructors but whose end serves the best interests of students.

Positive working relationships with other supervisors are important, too. Frequently, there is a need to confer with them about programming issues and making arrangements for teachers with dual classes in different departments. The AP never "undercuts" a colleague to benefit his/her own department's interests. The AP strives to resolve conflicts involving other supervisors, knowing that discord breeds hostility but that compromise will produce cooperation.

"Hey, where is Math 26A?"

The greatest genius will never be worth much if he pretends to draw exclusively from his own resources.

Johann Wolfgang von Goethe, author

Chapter Twelve

Community Relations

The school-parent relationship at the high school level has a weaker tradition than at the elementary school. Parental views of "the school" change as children get older. Many parents do not view the high school as being a part of the traditional school community because of its distance from the home and in the perception that an older child does not require the same degree of supervision given to a younger one. The greater impersonality of the high school population, its organizational complexity and emphasis upon academics, rather than upon early child development, produces considerable parental detachment. Yet, the high school years are critical for youngsters as are those at the elementary level. It is important therefore, that the parent-high school relationship be strengthened so that youngsters may achieve academic success. The first link between high school and home is often the result of student feedback of their teachers and school activities. Contact between home and school does not occur frequently enough unless some situation involving a youngster's classroom performance, a discipline or guidance problem, arises. What, then is the AP's role in helping bridge the "interaction gap" between community and school?

Narrowing the "interaction gap" can be formidable. The AP can help narrow the gap by promoting community awareness of the school program. At the start of each new term, I had department teachers distribute a "Course Requirement Contract" to their students at the first class meeting. The "contract" evolved of the need to connect families into a working relationship with their children's teachers. About 650 copies of the "contract" were distributed to students each term. A sample follows:

Edward F. Frenau, Principal
Foreign Language Department

Dwight E. Masterson, Assistant Principal, Supervision

COURSE REQUIREMENT CONTRACT IN FOREIGN LANGUAGES

You are to bring a pen to class daily. A replacement pen should also be available when needed. The teacher is not a source of pen replacement.

You will need a 3-ring looseleaf binder size 8 1/2 X 11 inches with an adequate amount of paper.

In your binder, a separate section should be provided for:

      1. Class section notes
      2. Homework

Homework Policy: You may miss 3 homework assignments, under unusual circumstances, each term. Each homework missed, up to 3, must be made up within 48 hours; no additional missing homework will be accepted without penalty. All homework is to be presented by the date due.

<u>Textbooks</u>: To be presented in class at the discretion of the teacher. Replacement of a book will be made only after payment for a book loss has been made.

<u>Absences:</u> All absences must be accounted for with a note from home and/or a doctor. You are responsible for all work missed. Notes are copied from classmates after class.

<u>Grading Policy</u>: To be announced by each teacher. Explanation should be kept in your notebook or at a safe place at home.

School policy states that no food of any kind is to be permitted in class. This includes gum, candy, soda, etc.

(Cut along this line and return signed)

Student Declaration:

    I have read and understand the class requirements and agree to abide by them. I further understand that my education is my responsibility.

_____

Student Signature

_____ _____

Date   Subject Class

Partnership Agreement:

    I/we have read and understand the above and agree to enter into a partnership with the faculty of John F. Kennedy High School in the education of my son/daughter and pledge to help in any way that I/we can.

_____

Date

_____

Parent/Guardian Signature

Approved: *Edward F. Frenau*

Edward F. Frenau, Principal

Other "connects" that help narrow the "interaction gap" occur during Open School Week, a Spring Conference, and PTA meetings. The latter is, however, poorly attended at the urban high school level. These conferences are helpful in offering parents an opportunity to meet teachers face to face to assess their children's academic progress, to discuss a problem, and/or to inquire about vocational opportunities and college admission. For many parents, the semi-annual visit may be the lone contact with the school and their perception of the school is often lasting. Brightly decorated hallways and clean classrooms, demonstrating student academic and community activities, are most helpful in being viewed as indicative of good student-teacher-administrative relationships.

Favorable school publicity resulting from coordinated school-wide effort assists to narrow the "interaction gap." Two positive vehicles are the department newsletter, published once or twice each semester, and the local news media. Editors have news space that needs to be filled before going to press and they can be very accommodating in printing school news. Announcements of department projects, student statistics, teacher achievements, school trips, highlights of curricular activities, and an educator's efforts to help place graduates in colleges or assist with vocational opportunities can help bond the school to the community. Interaction with community leaders in securing business support for academic/cultural events or interscholastic activities also strengthens the communal link to the school.

The Internet also links the community with the school. Schools have created their own web sites. If your school is not yet on-line, your input at the principal's administrative staff conference can serve as an avenue for change. A web site is a positive source of information that quickly links a family to their children's school.

Chapter Thirteen

Technology Education

Computer availability in the schools makes it incumbent upon educators to prepare youngsters with skills necessary for work and college. The NCLB Act maintains that a primary goal of *Education Through Technology (ED Tech)* is to teach children to use technological tools and to insure that teachers integrate technology into the curriculum to improve student achievement. The AP needs to make computer education an integral part of the department's curriculum. Chairpersons of social studies, the language arts, health education, art, and physical sciences must evolve goals that maximize computer competency across the curriculum's spectrum. Each student, by the time of graduation, should attain a working knowledge of software such as Microsoft "Word." Regrettably, typing instruction has all but disappeared from the high school curriculum. It should be "reinstated" as a component of computer education.

During the freshman year, youngsters should be given instruction in typing, and in their sophomore year introduced to word processing. This would include learning multiple operations in the preparation of writing assignments and in the production of computer generated presentations. In the junior year, written assignments would be broadened to include inclusion of footnoting and bibliographical citations. Youngsters with no computers at home should have PCs available to them during lunch and study periods in a school computer center. In that computer-center availability is usually conditional upon the school budget, monetary shortfalls could be alleviated by "tapping" federal sources under *ED Tech* and/or having the school administration undertake target marketing of the business community. By the senior year, students are encouraged to select an elective course titled *Independent Study*. This *Independent Study* elective provides a youngster with mentoring in order to complete an original research project. The resulting class grade, based upon a Department's assessment criteria, would be a good indicator of the student's literary/computer level of competency.

Ideally, cooperative teaching teams should be scheduled to train students in research writing; a language arts mentor, to assist with written English, and a subject teacher to monitor content. When budget constraints do not permit cooperative instruction for seniors, a teacher-advisor is programmed to counsel a select number of students during a single period each day. This period is programmed in common for both the instructor and the youngster opting for *Independent Study*. The number of students permitted in an *Independent Study* section are limited by a cutoff number each term.

My own experience with Independent Study evolved as a result of a conversation with the school Principal when he raised the issue of offering a course in art history to interested juniors. As a result, I and sixteen students were programmed for a seventh-period class. At our first meeting, my students were given a "handout" of course guidelines. The following is a sample of the guidelines:

Thomas Jefferson High School

M.L. Smith, Principal   B. Anker, AP (SUP) Academic Dept.

INDEPENDENT STUDY AT JEFFERSON

<u>Introduction:</u>
     Any Independent Study course, by nature, requires that the students give 100 percent of themselves. Independent Study requires that you meet all deadlines.
     Below, are specific requirements necessary for completion of Independent Study.

<u>Requirements:</u>
     1) You will be given a manila folder for the keeping of all assignments, memos, and notes. This folder is to be identified on the front cover, upper left corner, with your (print) <u>name, address, home telephone number, official class, course title</u>, and <u>instructor's name</u>. This folder is to be presented when meeting with me, your teacher.
     2) On the inside cover <u>(left side)</u> you are to <u>staple three sheets</u> of blank writing paper (8 1/2 x 11). Place the heading <u>Teacher's Comments and Assignments</u> at the top of the first page. The folder should look like this:

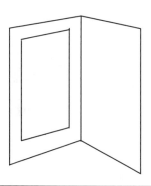

3) The class will meet daily in room 413 before undertaking a class period of research. You will meet with me personally once each week in room 413 for mentoring instructions. You are to appear with all your completed assignments. If you are absent, you will meet with me on the day of your return in room 107, <u>before period 1 begins</u>, to reschedule an appointment. A note from home explaining your absence must be presented. If no note is presented signed by parent or guardian, you will be marked absent for that day. More than two unexplained absences will result in failure and you will be dropped from Independent Study.

4) You may be issued a text and/or other additional materials for which you will complete book receipts. If the book/materials are lost, you will receive no course grade until they are paid for.

5) There are no exams in the course. You will, however, be asked to write an original research paper of personal choice. The paper may also reflect text and materials assigned for class. The final grade in the class will be determined by your paper's content, footnoting, bibliography, and English usage. The paper must be written <u>using a computer</u>. The minimum passing grade is 65.

(tear off)

I have read all of the above requirements for the Independent Study Program. I appreciate Jefferson's offer of self- study and acknowledge that I will give 100 percent effort to this partnership with both the instructor and the school. The course that I seek credit for is titled_____.

_____   _____
        Date   Pupil Signature (required)

_____   _____
        Date   Parent Signature
Approved: _____
                M.L. Smith, Principal

There were logistics to work out that first term. Each day I mentored 3-4 students by scheduled appointments while the others worked in-class or given permission to do their work in the school library. When assigned to the library they had to sign a special library log that I monitored or they were marked absent for the period. If on occasion I was absent, those scheduled for appointments were rescheduled upon my return to class. This was done during my office hour and during the student's study or part of his/her lunch period.

Preparing for tomorrow!

The difference between failure and success is doing a thing nearly right and doing it exactly right.

Edward Simmons, artist

Chapter Fourteen

Evaluating a Lesson

Imagine you are an Assistant Principal, Supervision and Administration, Science. You are about to observe Mr. Roberts, a second-year probationary teacher in your department, teaching a classroom lesson. What follows is a description of his class activities during a forty-minute period. As you read, evaluate the teacher's performance for its strengths and weaknesses.

Class: General Science 16
Period: 6, 12:20-1:00 P.M.
Class Level: Average ability **Register:** 33
Yesterday's topic: Earth's Atmosphere
Homework was assigned.

The bell rings at 12:20 P.M., signaling the beginning of period 6. Mr. Roberts is conversing with two youngsters at his desk. Students are seated and talking to one another.

12:25 P.M.

Mr. Roberts: "Open your notebooks and copy the board work. For homework, study air pressure and do the first three problems at the end of the chapter. Steve, come up to the desk and try to push this egg into the milk bottle. Don't crush it!"

Steve fails to get the egg to go into the bottle.

Mr. Roberts: "Mary, would you please come up and help me."

The teacher lights a small piece of paper which he drops into the bottle and asks Mary to place the egg at the top of the bottle's mouth. The egg fails to enter the bottle.

Mr. Roberts: "Well, if you don't succeed, try, try again."

The experiment is repeated, using a larger piece of paper. The egg enters the bottle. A girl raises her hand, but yells out, "Mr. Roberts, can I go to the bathroom?" Mr. Roberts replies, "Take the pass, Jennifer. You know where it is."

Mr. Roberts: "Why did the egg go into the bottle, Steve?" Steve haltingly replies, "The heat made the egg small enough to fit."

Mr. Roberts: "Mindy?"

Mindy, startled, says, "I'm not sure, teacher. Maybe because the flame used the air up inside the bottle and the air outside pushed the egg in?"

Mr. Roberts: "Anyone else?"

A boy, row three, seat three, raises his hand. "Yes, Peter," says Mr. Roberts. Jennifer returns, pushes the classroom door shut causing a loud bang, waves to a friend, and takes her seat. "Yes, Peter," repeats the teacher. "There is a difference in pressure. The outside pressure is greater," answers Peter.

Mr. Roberts: "Why did I light the piece of paper?"

A youngster in the 4th row, 5th seat, calls out, "The fire consumed all the air, producing a vacuum that pulled the air in." The teacher does not respond. He turns to the chalkboard and writes, "How does heat affect air pressure?"

Mr. Roberts: "Sal, read what I have written on the board." Sal reads the question from the board. The teacher says, "Let's discuss this. What is air pressure? What causes air pressure?" There are no responses. The teacher points to a girl sitting in row one, seat two. Startled, she asks, "Can I go to the bathroom?" "Not until you answer the question," says the teacher. The girl answers, "Heat." The teacher responds, "How?" The girl says, "I have to go bad, Mr. Roberts." The teacher replies, "Answer first, then you can go." The girl responds, "Heat took up all the air?"

Mr. Roberts: "We are talking about air pressure. What is it? What causes it? Mark?"

Mark, sitting in row six, seat five, answers, "Maybe it's the weight of the air itself." "Can I go now?" calls out the girl in row one, seat two. "Go where?" asks the teacher, forgetfully. "To the bathroom," says the girl. "O.K., but hurry back," replies the teacher. The teacher turns from the class and writes on the board, "Air pressure is caused by the weight of the air itself." He draws a diagram of the earth and its surrounding atmosphere.

12:40 P.M.

Mr. Roberts: "What from outer space gives us a clue to the atmosphere and what do we observe?"

A boy volunteers a response. "Meteors."

Mr. Roberts: "How?"

"They look like a fireball," says Harold. The teacher asks, "When?" Harold replies, "When they hit the atmosphere."

Mr. Roberts: "How high is this?"

There is no student response.

Mr. Roberts: "Imagine 22,000 miles of air over you. This exerts air pressure. Suppose you had a square inch of air. How much would it weigh? Amy?"

Amy thinks for a moment. "How can it weigh anything at all? A square inch is flat!"

Mr. Roberts: "I mean if it's a column of air one square inch wide and very tall? Amy?"

Mark calls out, "It would weigh 15 pounds."

Mr. Roberts: "Not exactly. Actually it would weigh 14.7 pounds."

The teacher holds a sheet of paper in his hand, tells the class that it measures 8 inches by 10 inches and asks, "What is the total force on this paper?" The teacher points to a student in row four, seat one and says, "Come to the board and show us how to measure this."

Lillian appears reluctant but rises from her seat, goes to the board and writes:

$$8 \times 10 = \quad 80 \text{ sq. in.}$$
$$80 \times 15 = 1,200 \text{ sq. in.}$$

The teacher looks at Lillian's calculations, erases "sq. in." after 1,200 and writes "lbs." He offers no explanation.

12:45P.M.

Mr. Roberts: "Why can I lift this paper?"

Lillian volunteers a response and answers, "The pressure is the same on all sides."

The teacher goes to the board and writes, "Air pressure is equal in all directions." The instructor invites two volunteers to join him in demonstrating the use of Magdeberg hemispheres (a device used to measure air pressure). One student assists by pumping the air out of the device. Mr. Roberts asks the volunteers to now try to pull the sphere apart. They can't. The teacher calls upon two girls from the back of the room to come forward while he slowly opens a valve of the connecting spheres (allowing air back in). The girls easily pull the spheres apart.

Mr. Roberts: "Why couldn't the spheres be pulled apart before?"

Mark yells out, "There was more air inside than outside." Lillian responds, "There was more air outside than inside."

Mr. Roberts: "Removal of air caused a partial vacuum. What have you learned about air pressure so far?"

Jose, row five, seat one raises his hand, is called upon, and reads the statements from the board that the teacher has previously written.

Mr. Roberts: "All right. Copy that into your notebooks." The teacher sets up a convection of air apparatus and lights its candle.

Mr. Roberts: "Sal, what do you observe?"

Sal responds, "I'm still copying into my notebook." The teacher appears somewhat annoyed.

Mr. Roberts: "Pay attention, Sal. Cindy, what do you see?"

Cindy answers, "The smoke goes in one side and out the other."

The teacher asks, "Why?"

Cindy responds, "I don't know."

12:56 P.M.

Mr. Roberts: "Anybody?" There is no response.

The teacher extinguishes the candle and demonstrates that the smoke no longer enters the box but shows that when the candle is lit again the smoke enters one side and goes out the other.

The teacher calls upon Jackie. "Jackie, what are you doing?"

Jackie answers, "Looking at my textbook."

Mr. Roberts calls upon Tommy. "What does this demonstration prove, Tommy?"

Tommy responds, "The burning candle pushes air up."

"O.K.," says the teacher. "What else, Andrew?"

Andrew, in a muted voice, answers, "The burning candle made the air pressure less, and therefore it could escape easier."

Mr. Roberts: "Harriet?"

Harriet, in apparent discomfort, asks, "Mr. Roberts, can I go to the bathroom?"

The teacher presses on. "Samuel?"

Samuel, slouching back in his seat, says, "I think Tommy is right. The layer of air over a chimney keeps the smoke in when the candle is not lit. When the candle is lit, the air becomes heated and expands and therefore creates less pressure and the smoke goes out."

Mr. Roberts goes to the chalkboard and writes.
1. Hot air rises.
2. Cool air moves toward warm air.
3. Cool air exerts more pressure.

A student raises his hand.
Mr. Roberts: "Lenny, you have a question?"
Lenny says, "I've just looked at my textbook and it says that when a balloon is heated, the pressure increases and causes the balloon to break. You wrote on the board, 'Cool air exerts more pressure.' Which is correct?"

The bell rings, signaling the end of the period.

Questions For You To Consider

1. Can you identify at least two of Mr. Robert's instructional strengths using evidence from the lesson description?
2. Can you identify significant weaknesses of Mr. Robert's lesson performance and propose one or more constructive suggestions to assist him with eliminating these weaknesses?
3. At a post-observation conference, what two immediate weaknesses would you highlight?
4. What supervisory program would you prescribe for Mr. Roberts to assist him in overcoming these weaknesses?

An Evaluation of Mr. Roberts's Lesson

Mr. Roberts appears to be a motivated teacher but lacks basic understanding of classroom practice and teaching methodology. The teacher attempted to motivate classroom interest with a series of science experiments and appeared cognizant of the need for student socialization in lesson activities. Asking Mary, for example, to assist with a class demonstration was a positive socializing decision. However, Mr. Roberts's weak teaching performance is typical of most novice instructors. The following weaknesses are offered for consideration:

The teacher demonstrated poor classroom management. He failed to set priorities for launching necessary basic classroom operations to achieve classroom stability. The period began at 12:20 P.M., yet, the teacher did not begin lesson preliminaries until 12:25 P.M. The word "Aim" was not placed on the chalkboard in anticipation of eliciting it from the class at some point during the lesson; the Aim was never elicited nor was one written on the chalkboard! The instructor did not place a homework assignment upon the board at a customary location for students to see and copy. In addition, Mr. Roberts made no reference to, nor did he collect, the previous night's homework assignment. His verbalization of a vague new homework assignment, "Study air pressure and do the first three problems at the end of the chapter," without indicating the assignment's page numbers, ill-served youngsters that may not have heard it, or the occasional latecomer who did not see an assignment on the board. In his haste to initiate the lesson, Mr. Roberts forgot to take the daily attendance, thus violating a primary legal requirement common to most school districts across the nation. The aforementioned weaknesses could have been avoided had the teacher adopted basic management routines for launching his lesson. Mr. Roberts failed to bring his class to order and readiness!

Mr. Roberts needs to establish clearly defined rules for the use of the pass in his classroom. Personal classroom experience dictates that the pass not be issued, the exception being an emergency, for the first and last ten minutes of a period. In addition, no more than three students should be allowed to leave the room during any single period to avoid a "domino-like effect" in pass use. The room pass should be placed at a strategic location so that a student may exit and re-enter with minimum disruption. Any student yelling out for the pass forfeits its use. Students should also be conditioned to raising a hand when they wish to leave the room.

The instructor failed to develop his lesson. Mr. Roberts did not initiate a review of previous subject content aimed at providing continuity with the day's lesson. Had he asked a student volunteer to summarize some aspect of previous subject content from class notes, it would have aided him in setting the stage for the lesson's development. Mr. Roberts lost an opportunity to establish an ongoing content dialogue with his class. Instead, Mr. Roberts undertook several science experiments without first preparing the lesson's foundation. This was obvious when he asked Steve to "try to push this egg into the milk bottle don't crush it," before properly introducing the objective of Steve's action. It was at this point that the instructor lost the class. Mr. Roberts' demonstration technique was an instructional failure for several reasons.

1. He did not inform his students of scientifically established content. A youngster in the 4th row, 5th seat stated that, "removal of air from the container produced a vacuum." Mr. Roberts, in turn, did not acknowledge this student's response as correct or incorrect but moved on to another matter. He did this throughout the lesson.

2. By not using accepted scientific methodology, the teacher hindered student understanding of "cause and effect" relationships. Mr. Roberts's use of the Magdeberg hemispheres, without first explaining the function of the apparatus, and asking the class to "imagine 22,000 miles of air over you" and a vague reference to air pressure being "not 15 pounds but actually 14.7 pounds" (without properly explaining and stating this in terms of pounds per sq. in.) were examples of the teacher's ignorance of lesson development.

The instructor's poor questioning technique was similarly a contributing factor in the lesson's lack of cohesiveness and development. Mr. Roberts asked "vague" and often "one-word" or "guess" questions, such as, "Why did I light the piece of paper?" "What have we learned about air pressure so far?" and "How?" that compounded student confusion. He asked double or multiple questions such as "We are talking about air pressure. What is it? What causes it? Mark?" and "What from outer space gives us a clue to the atmosphere and what do we observe?" It would have been preferable that the latter two questions been asked as single questions. Mr. Roberts may have stimulated class interest, and caused less confusion, by restating his question, had he asked, "How do you explain air exerting pressure upon us?" then pausing 5 to 8 seconds so that students could "internalize" the question before responding. Asking a specific student to reply immediately to a question diminished the "internalizing" process and class involvement. The second of his two questions could have been rephrased as "Can someone describe the layers of our atmosphere that a meteor must penetrate before hitting earth?" Had the teacher planned a series of preliminary questions in order to establish the lesson's foundation, and had he introduced factual concepts followed by several pivotal questions, he could have established a proper sequence of scientific principles.

Mr. Roberts failed to use the chalkboard as an effective teaching tool. The teacher asked that students copy the board work. But what were they to copy? We know that later in the lesson, Sal read a board statement to which Mr. Roberts responded, "Lets discuss this." But what was to be discussed? The teacher never clarified! Was it the first question, "What is air pressure?" or the second, "What causes air pressure?" The instructor's chalkboard notes lacked clarity, cohesiveness, and scientific accuracy when he wrote, 1. Hot air rises. 2. Cool air moves toward warm air. 3. Cool air exerts more pressure. The latter two statements were incorrect and led Lenny to "cross-examine" the teacher. This event raises issue as to whether there was a teaching error or a lack in the teacher's subject knowledge. Mr. Roberts had no meaningful chalkboard notes under appropriate topic headings that could have united content information. There were no medial or final summaries. These factors contributed to the lesson's lack of structure and order. The teacher also appeared to have lost all sense of class time. This, too, assured the lesson's failure.

Mr. Roberts has numerous instructional problems. At a post-observation conference, I would inform the teacher of my observations and offer him assistance. I would, in conjunction with the teacher, prepare a plan to uplift his classroom skills. Mr. Roberts's two most pressing weaknesses are his poor management procedures and his need for good lesson planning. Mr. Roberts' acceptance of an assistance plan would be an important precondition for undertaking a skills-building program.

I would take small steps at first to build teacher confidence, being careful not to overwhelm the instructor with multiple teaching components at once. In addition, I would arrange for his visits to my classes as well as those of other department members. The goal of the visitation process would be to help the instructor discover a variety of teaching styles for meaningful instruction. I would also visit his classroom frequently, to offer constructive feedback. A "buddy" would be assigned to the teacher for assistance when Mr. Roberts was of immediate need.

Mishaps are like knives, which either serve us or cut us, as we grasp them by the blade or handle.

Herman Melville, author

Chapter Fifteen

Problem Solving

What follows are a series of problem-related memos that you, the AP, might receive upon occasion. Outline the steps you might pursue for solving each memo problem.

Memo #1

March 23, 20__

To: Mr. Jerry Marks, AP

The students of French 234 ask you to remove Mr. Horrid, our present subject teacher. We have to take the State exam in French at the end of this term, so we really need a good teacher.

During the past week he has gotten angry at the slightest things and leaves the room. We need a teacher who will teach us so we can pass our French exam.

Thank you.

Yours truly,
French Class 234

Memo #2

January 14, 20__

Dear Ms. Robbins,

As you know, this is my first year as a teacher. I am having several problems with my teaching duties and am not sure how to best handle the situations facing me. I have three preparations for my five classes. I am daily confronted by the same latecomers. I also believe my class discipline and cutting problems are due to a lack of appropriate materials.

I would appreciate your assistance.

Sincerely,
Jane Miserable

Memo #3

February 3, 20__

Dear Dr. Roth,

I have successfully taught Advanced Placement Mathematics for the past three years. The majority of my students have attained outstanding grades and credit toward their college degrees. My class attendance has been second to none. In addition, a review of my observation reports will substantiate my claim.

I do not know why this class was taken from me and given to another with less teaching experience. He is really unqualified to teach Advanced Placement having taken his last college course more than twelve years ago and lacks familiarity with new methods in mathematics instruction. It is obvious to me that our youngsters will suffer if I am not assigned as the Advanced Placement teacher.

I eagerly await your response.

Sincerely,
Lynn Begood

Memo #4

For Mr. Shelton, AP
Time 12:25   Date 4/23/03

WHILE YOU WERE OUT

M Mother of Alicia Rodriguez (Class 211)
Phone 693-456-4123

TELEPHONED	X	URGENT	X
PLEASE CALL	X	WANTS TO SEE YOU	
WILL CALL AGAIN		CAME TO SEE YOU	
RETURNED YOUR CALL			

MESSAGE Parent very upset. Claims that daughter's 3rd period teacher is prejudiced and wants her transferred or she will file a complaint with the Board of Ed.

Irma Jones, Secretary

Memo #5

From: Rich Boulton, Junior Advisor
To: Dr. Sally Redford, AP
Subject: End-term rating

Dear Dr. Redford,

   In preparation for the end of the term, I've been checking Junior records and have discovered a problem with one student who appears rather troublesome. It seems that Mr. Shepfield, in your department, has given a grade of 90 to a student named Gloria Brighteyes but all other subject teachers have failed her because of excessive absence.
   Could you please check this out? Thanks.

Memo #6

September 15, 20__

Dear Dr. Redford,
   I am going insane! My 4th period class in Advanced Placement American History has 41 kids and I keep getting new admits, daily. They enter the class at the beginning of the period and start to argue over seats. It takes me more than 15 minutes each day to try to organize this class before taking attendance. Some sit on windowsills while others kneel at my desk in an attempt to take notes. I don't have enough chairs for all these kids. I know this is the only section being taught this term, but something has to be done! HELP!!!!!!

Robin Hanks

POSSIBLE SOLUTIONS TO PROBLEMS

Memo #1

I would inform the teacher that I will be visiting his French 234 class, informally, shortly. During my visitation, I would randomly examine five or six student notebooks for lesson Aims, medial and final summaries, French vocabulary, and/or grammatical rules, model sentences, and homework assignments. I would also ask several youngsters from the class to visit me during a part of their lunch period (I would prepare hand-written passes for them before coming to the class) at a prearranged location. The interviews would be to fact-find and substantiate, if any, class-room/teacher problems. If I determine, after my classroom observation and student interviews, that there are sufficient reasons to pursue their complaint further, I would ask the instructor to meet with me.

At our meeting, I would examine several of the teacher's recent lesson plans to evaluate whether or not there are shortcomings with lesson preparation. If the lesson plans reveal significant weakness and confirm several of my negative classroom observations, if any, I would inform him of student complaints. I would ask him to respond, in particular, to the accusation that he "got angry and left the room," an act prohibited to a teacher without his/her being relieved by a school aide. After listening carefully to the teacher's explanation regarding the complaints and having discussed my findings with him, a Chair-teacher plan would be necessary to eliminate any continuing instructional problems. This meeting would be documented for future reference.

Memo #2

Ms. Miserable's difficulties reflect those of many first-year teachers. I would explain to her, during an informal meeting, that every effort is made to keep the number of individual teacher preps to a minimum but that it is not always feasible. Reasons for this occurring can be large numbers of incoming ninth-grade students that require the creation of several additional class sections, or a result of several veteran teachers having time-compensated positions that make them unavailable for full instructional loads, so that their classes have to be redirected to others.

I would stress the need for good lesson planning. I would review with Ms. Miserable her present class management and preventive discipline techniques. I would ask her to informally invite me to visit her classes in order to update her progress and to offer assistance. I would inform the teacher that class discipline and cutting problems are usually the result of poor lesson planning, poor implementation and a lack of preventive discipline measures. Her situation may also require that Ms. Miserable visit classrooms of more experienced teachers to become better acquainted with instructional techniques.

I would want a clarification as to what Ms. Miserable means by a "lack of appropriate materials." If shortages exist, I would make every effort to accommodate the teacher. In the meantime, I would ask her to notify the homes of frequent latecomers and class cutters and to arrange, if necessary, for parent-teacher conferences. I would also assign a "buddy teacher" to assist Ms. Miserable.

Memo #3

Lynn Begood appears to be a teacher with a "bruised" ego. She fails to understand that she does not have province over a right to teach Advanced Placement Mathematics. I would acknowledge her successes, but inform her that I have an obligation to all members of the department to rotate this class. In that Ms. Begood is concerned with the assigned teacher's lack of familiarity with "new methods," and that students would "suffer" as a result of it, I would encourage Ms. Begood to remain involved with the Advanced Placement class by offering her expertise to the teacher. I would arrange a meeting of Ms. Begood, the newly assigned instructor, and myself, to explore ideas for making the Advanced Placement class a continued success. My action would demonstrate confidence in Ms. Begood, provide her with an opportunity for input in an area of interest, and assist the new, but less experienced, instructor, to become better acquainted with the requisites for undertaking this class.

Memo #4

This message can be an AP's nightmare! I would handle the matter with empathy, efficacy, and communicative skill. My first step would be to contact the mother as quickly as possible. I would inform her that I'm sorry she is upset. I would listen carefully to what she says and record it with date and time of the contact. I would read the complaint back to the parent to avoid a possible misunderstanding. I would try to allay the mother's anger by assuring her I would get back to her shortly. I would then proceed with Step 2.

I would speak with the girl to determine if she is indeed having a problem in her 3rd period class and cross-checking her comments with the mother's complaint. Are they both in agreement regarding the complaint? If affirmative, I would "dig deeper," by asking the girl to elaborate upon specific events, places, dates, and possible witnesses. If the girl's tale is, however, different from that of the mother, or there are no indications of teacher prejudice, I would have the girl write her version of the perceived problem, if one exists. I would investigate whether other youngsters have made similar complaints against the teacher in question, with the Guidance Office and other Assistant Principals. I would then proceed with Step 3.

I would meet with the teacher and document the conference. I would inform the teacher of the mother's and/or the student's complaints. The teacher would have the right of rebuttal to any accusation. If I was suspect of the instructor's explanation, I would inform the Principal of my suspicions, and seek his advice as to how he/she might want me to proceed with the situation. If, however, the teacher's explanation was plausible and there was reason to believe the complaint frivolous, or the result of a misunderstanding, I would ask the teacher to meet with the mother and daughter to seek a resolution. I would contact the mother, inform her of my findings, and invite her and her daughter to a parent-teacher meeting in my office.

Memo #5

Before meeting with Mr. Shepfield, I would review all of the instructor's class lists for "inflated" grades. I would check the attendance of Gloria Brighteyes in the Attendance Office, record the dates absent from school and speak with her teachers about her performance and attendance in their classes. If there was an error, I would notify Mr. Boulton, the Junior Advisor, of it. If there was no error, I would ask Mr. Shepfield to bring his grade and attendance book to a meeting with me.

I would cross-check the student's absences with those in Mr. Shepfield's attendance book. If there were inconsistencies, I would question Mr. Shepfield about his record-keeping methods and his possible inflation of grades for excessively absent youngsters. Mr. Shepfield would be given every consideration. I would, however, advise him of his legal responsibilities as a classroom teacher and of the seriousness in faulty and inaccurate student record keeping. I would be resolute that he update student attendance records for accuracy and make necessary grade corrections. I, and the Grade Advisor, would be informed of any changes. I would be cognizant of monitoring attendance and final grades for discrepancies in future semesters. This meeting would be documented.

Memo #6

Receipt of such a memo, especially during the early days of a new term, is not unusual. The memo reflects teacher anxiety resulting from classroom overcrowding. The event requires immediate action by the AP.

I would secure the teacher's list of names of youngsters signed into the class. A quick check in the Program Office of names initially registered for the class, against those on the teacher list, should reveal students that do not belong. A program change by the Program Office would be necessary to place those not belonging in the 4th period Advanced Placement American History into their correct subject classes. However, if those registered for the class cross-check correctly with the names appearing on the teacher's class list, than there is an error in limiting class size. How should exclusion from this class be determined when all the youngsters pre-registered for it in the previous term? In fairness to all, I would assign those to the class based on their earliest registration dates. Those not immediately placed would be pledged first entry the following term or when the course was next offered. These names would be kept on file in my department office.

Conclusion

This book is written to guide a new Assistant Principal in making a smooth transition into the position of a secondary school supervisor. The book's contents should not be viewed as absolute. Its chapters are designed with the intent of addressing important issues of supervision. They do not depict, nor were they meant to portray, the gamut of an AP's daily duties, but only to provide insight into the functions of a department, to establish an environment for democratic leadership, and to foster positive human relationships. A special consideration has been given to the AP's role in staff development. In most cases, an Assistant Principal has achieved his/her position after many years of classroom experience. Although his/her instructional mastery continues to play a vital role, other personal qualities are necessary for supervisory success.

The chairperson is viewed as a school leader. Yet an ability to lead does not manifest itself until one gains the confidence of one's peers. There are individuals who embrace, whether consciously or unconsciously, an elitist mentality upon appointment as Assistant Principals. Such types frequently prove to be ineffective supervisors. To gain the assurance of others means demonstrating respect for them, listening to what they say, assisting them when called upon to do so, showing consideration for their special needs, and being sincere when making personal commitments.

The Chair confidently sets goals, knows what he/she wishes to achieve, and draws willingly upon the resources of others to attain them. He/she similarly delegates authority to department members and doesn't interfere with their actions as long as policy decided upon is carried out. The AP markets ideas to others by communicating skillfully and frequently to achieve a "final sale;" these ideas are staff shared and criticized, modified until deemed desirable, and put into practice.

The Assistant Principal is a risk taker! His/her advocacy of instructional experimentation inspires teachers to be innovative but pragmatic in their classrooms. As an educational leader, the AP desires to be informed of classroom successes so that they may be shared with others. Establishing a department environment in which teacher creativity is esteemed rather than given pro forma "lip service" serves as a potent force for uplifting classroom instruction. This instills staff trust while generating a preference for educational change and non-maintenance of the status quo.

Bibliography

Baughman, M. Dale, *Administration and Supervision of the Modern Secondary School*, (Parker Publishing Co: New York, 1969)

Douglas, Harl R., Bent, Rudyard K. and Boardman, Charles W., *Democratic Supervision in Secondary Schools*, 2nd ed. (Houghton Mifflin: Boston, 1961)

Glickman, Carl D., *Leadership in Learning: How to Help Teachers Succeed*, (Association for Supervision and Curriculum Development: Alexandria, 2002)

Glanz, Jeffrey, *Finding Your Leadership Style: A Guide for Educators*, (Association for Supervision and Curriculum Development: Alexandria, 2002)

Kraut, Harvey, *Teaching and the Art of Successful Classroom Management: A How-to Guidebook for Teachers in Secondary Schools*, 3rd ed. (Aysa Publishing, Inc: New York, 2000)

Oliva, Peter F. and Pawles, George E., *Supervision for Today's Schools*, 6th ed. (Wiley: New York, 2001)

Pajak, Edward, *Honoring Diverse Teaching Styles: A Guide for Supervisors*, (Association for Supervision and Curriculum Development: Alexandria, 2003)

Secretary Paige Unveils New Testing Guide for Families, Schools and Communities, 13 February, 2002 U.S. Department of Education

Zepeda, Sally, *Instructional Supervision: Applying Tools and Concepts*, (Eye On Education: Larchmont, 2002)

Preparation, preparation, and more preparation!!

Forms: Teaching Staff

FORM A: AN OPENING TERM CHECKLIST FOR TEACHERS

Date_____

I have secured the following necessary and immediate items from my supervisor for the opening of the new term:

- ❑ My term program
- ❑ Subject text/texts
- ❑ Restroom key
- ❑ Opening day attendance lists
- ❑ A calendar of lessons
- ❑ Uniform homework sheets (if available)
- ❑ Attendance and record-keeping book
- ❑ Staff information booklet
- ❑ VCR inventory list
- ❑ Six absentee lessons with instructions
- ❑ Discipline referral forms
  (school form if available)
- ❑ School stationery and envelopes
- ❑ Content material (maps, test tubes,
  a chalkboard compass, etc.)
- ❑ Chalk, eraser and class pass

FORM B: CLASS SEATING CHART FOR TEACHERS

SEATING CHART

FORM C: A HOME CONTACT LETTER

John Brown High School
432 Franklin Street
Philadelphia, Pennsylvania 97100
Phone (326) 973-4200

Date_____

Mr./Ms._____

_____

_____

Dear Parent:

I am sorry to advise you that your son/daughter of class_____ may fail for the term for the following reasons:

---poor attendance   ---missing homework
---cutting class   ---lacks motivation
---absent on test days   ---is unprepared
---is late to class   ---poor test grades
---fails to hand-in assignments on time   ---lacks self control
                                          ----other_____

Please discuss the above checked items with your son/daughter. I am available to meet with you. Please call the above number to arrange a school appointment.

It is hoped that this matter can be resolved as quickly as possible.

Sincerely,

Joyce Smith, AP

Additional comments

FORM D: INTER-SCHOOL MEMO

John Adams Junior High School
1714 Riverdale Avenue
Houston, Texas 89132

Date_____

To:_____

From:_____

Topic:_____

Dear_____:

_____
_____
_____
_____
_____
_____
_____
_____
_____
_____

Sincerely,

FORM E: INTER-SCHOOL DISCIPLINE REFERRAL

Date_____

To: _____
From: _____
Re: (student's name and class)

Dear_____:

Description of Complaint:

_____

_____

_____

_____

_____

_____

_____

_____

_____

_____

_____

_____

_____

Sincerely,

FORM F: EXCESSIVE ABSENCE FROM CLASS

John Smith High School
2001 Sycamore Road
Santa Fe, New Mexico 87293

_____20__

Dear Parent/Guardian:

Your son/daughter_____ has
been absent several times in (state the month). I have attempted to
contact you but cannot locate a working telephone number.

Would you be so kind as to call me at:

Telephone #(123) 456-7889, extension #15, during the hour
7:30-8:30 AM.

Thank you.

Sincerely,

John Smith, AP

FORM G: EXCESSIVE ABSENCE FROM CLASS

Mary Jones Memorial High School
1155 Michigan Avenue
Flint, Michigan 56478

Date_____

Dear Parent/Guardian:

We regret to inform you that your son/daughter_____has
not been attending classes regularly. Continuous absence from
subject class_____can lead to failure and a delay of
graduation.

Please discuss this matter with your son/daughter. For additional
information please contact me, between the hours
_____daily, at (274) 789-1234.

Very truly yours,

Rachel Smith, AP

FORM H: NOTIFICATION OF SUBJECT FAILURE

R.W. Rathbone Junior High School
1865 Rose Lane
Buffalo, New York 14538

Date_____

Dear Parent/Guardian:

Please be advised that your son/daughter_____ has failed subject_____ for this marking period. Would you be so kind as to discuss this with your son/daughter.

Continued failure may result in having your child's graduation delayed.

If I may be of service to you in some way, please do not hesitate to call me at (343) 678-1234 between the hours of 8:45-9:20 A.M. If I am unavailable when you call, please leave a message and I will contact you shortly.

Sincerely,

Janet Bright, AP

131

FORM H: NOTIFICATION OF INCOMPLETE ACADEMIC WORK

Date_____

Dear Parent/Guardian:

We wish to inform you that your son/daughter will not be permitted to attend graduation _____20__, until he/she satisfactorily completes all previously failed or deficient academic work taken during the Fall/Spring 20__.

The faculty of _____looks forward to greeting you at graduation in June, 20__.

If you should have any questions, please call Mr._____ at _____ between the hours of 8:45-10:00 A.M.

Sincerely,

Assistant Principal

INDEX

A

B

C

Q

R

S

Notes

Notes

Notes

Notes

Notes

Order Form

Please forward the following order for ***The Assistant Principal and the Art of Successful Department Management***: **ISBN**: **0-9640602-5-6**:
Number of books:_____($19.95 each) Canada ($25.95)

Organization name: _____

Name: (please print)_____

Address: _____

City:_____ State:_____ Zip:_____

Sales tax:
Please add 8.63% for books shipped in New York State.

Shipping:
Book rate: <u>$2.50</u> for the first book and <u>$1.75</u> for each additional book.
Please permit 3-4 weeks for postal delivery.
Air Mail: <u>$8.00</u> per book.

Payment:
___ Check
___ Money Order

Please forward book orders to:

> **Aysa Publishing, Inc.**
> **P.O. Box 131556**
> **Staten Island, New York 10313**
> **U.S.A.**

For inquiries or additional information: **Phone & Fax (718) 370-3201**
I understand that I may return this book for a full refund, anytime, if I am not totally satisfied as long as the book is in good condition and still in print.